Ground
in
Eternity

Jenna Hastelow

Published by Seraph Creative

GROUND IN ETERNITY

Jenna Hastelow
Interior Illustrations by Jani Rättyä
Copyright © 2024

New International Version (NIV): Scripture quotations marked "NIV" Blue Letter Bible https://www.blueletterbible.org/ unless otherwise stated.

As is the Strongs concordance for the Hebrew and Greek, From the Blue Letter Bible.

Published by Seraph Creative in 2024

United States / United Kingdom / South Africa / Australia

www.seraphcreative.org

Contents

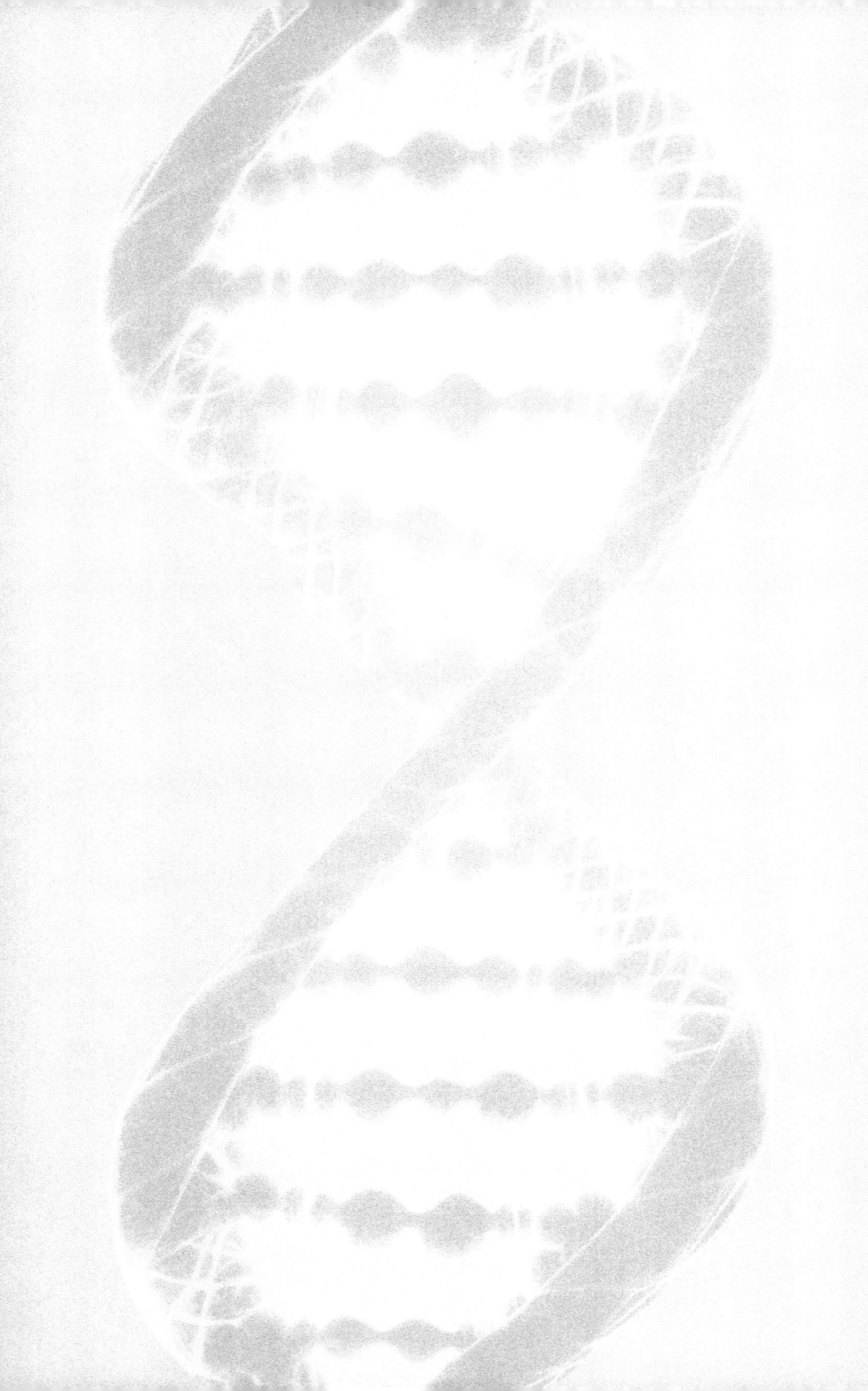

DEDICATED TO:

Ground in Eternity is dedicated to; all who struggle to believe God is good, to those who have been wounded and traumatised by religion, and to the next generation. You are seen, heard and loved.

It is also dedicated to Holy Spirit, without you I can do nothing. And finally but not lastly it is dedicated to the countless individuals who have loved me, supported me and been Christ to me, without you I would not be who I am now, thank you. I love the body of Christ, we are one.

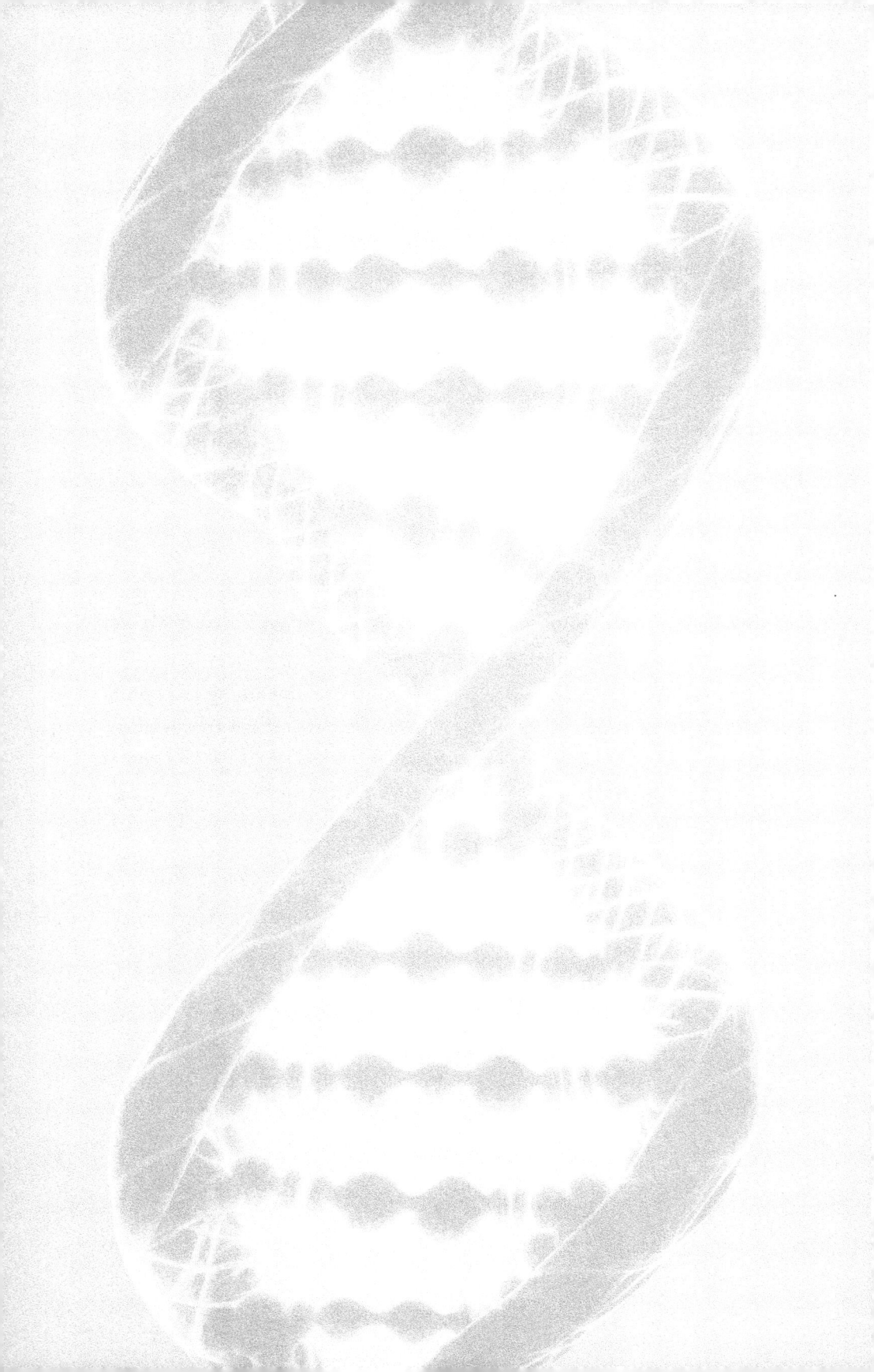

INTRODUCTION

In the beginning God. God is the beginning of all, whether we think of God as another being; impersonal or personal or we think of ourselves as a god this seems to be the essence of life and questions surrounding life. Sitting on the bus a few years ago I saw a sign that read, "Turn your heart into a temple of fire." I literally started burning, for I knew this sign to be true, we are meant to be a temple of fire. These bodies house something greater than flesh and bones, they house spirit, they house the eternal. The sign was advertising yoga classes however for me the sign was advertising an invitation from Holy Spirit. Would I let myself be a temple of fire? Would I embody the fire of love, would I embody God? I can believe in a God of love or not. I can believe in a creator or in nothing and for this simple mind of mine it takes more courage for me to believe in nothing than it does to believe in a supreme being. In fact, it freaks me out to have to conclude I am here by evolutionary chance and my existential questions remain unanswered. I did once, for one day and I didn't survive it. I ran back to the shelter of faith, despite the fact that I felt God was an angry, demanding being and I wasn't at all connected to this God. I grew up in a Christian home, my parents were found by Jesus the year I turned five. I had theoretical knowledge of God but did I know God or even like that being, I wasn't so sure.

It is at the age of seventeen that I face these questions despite having been baptised at eleven years old in good Baptist tradition. I turned then at the brink of adulthood to address my most pressing questions. Who am I? Why am I here? What is the point of it all? One of my favorite songs at the age of fifteen was *Creep* sung at that time by the band Radiohead.[1]

---

[1]Due to copyright issues I can't quote the lyrics but I do encourage you to look them up to understand the feeling. I will mention other songs in this manner also.

This was teenage longing in all its glory and yes I use that word deliberately. These longings for affirmation, purpose, and belonging are glorious, they are right. They deserve an answer. The cries of justice rising from the lips of adolescents are the most important cries on this planet and they must never be silenced, why? Because in these cries lies the very heart of God.

You are worthy, our Lord and God, to receive glory and honor and power, for you created all things, and by your will they were created and have their being. Revelation 4:11

This for me is the bottom line. It is God's will I am here. This for me is a thousand times more comforting than the big bang. Let it be known from the start. I need God. "Religion is a crutch" it has been said, I might agree with that. However the person of God is a different story, oh yes, let this person be my crutch, my biggest crutch, in fact, more than that I unashamedly let go of trusting myself. God is not just my crutch, God is my security blanket and the warm, soft bed I fall into regularly. God is my comforter and my friend. God is so much more than these things but for now as a starting point I wanted to share how honoured I am to have found such love and warmth in God despite the fact God is more powerful and greater than what I could possibly hope to convey or understand.

In the beginning, God created... and He said it was good. And then after he[2] had created humanity, namely Adam and Eve. God said they were very good.

So God created mankin in his own image, <u>in the image of God he created them; male and female he created them.</u>[3] Genesis 1:27

God saw all that he had made, and it was very good. And there was evening, and there was morning—the sixth day. Genesis 1:31

Look at the underlined part above, I would like to make clear from the beginning that I don't believe God is "he", neither do I think God is "she", God is outside gender. God is transcendent. The dictionary definition of transcendent is: exceeding usual limits, extending or lying beyond the limits of ordinary experience, being beyond comprehension, universally applicable or significant .[4]

---

[2]Scripture does not capitalise pronouns referring to God, for ease of reading I will be following the same formatting.

[3]Underlined for emphasis

[4]https://www.merriam-webster.com/dictionary/transcendent

However because English tradition uses male pronouns I will use "he" here. In the Finnish language third person personal pronouns do not define gender, one word is used "hän". How great it would be if I could use hän? However, since this is written in English not Finnish I will use both he and she as the pronoun for God where I deem appropriate.

Read the above verses again. You are very good! You are not bad, unworthy, evil, etc. God declared at creation, humanity to be very good, and yet we in some places in the Christian community have departed a long way from this declaration of truth. We may 'sin'-miss the mark. However we are good, God says so. The first mention of the word sin is in Genesis 4:7. The Hebrew root word is châţâ, which means; to miss, to miss the way, miss the mark, to lose oneself. Jesus came so we would be able to; find the way, hit the mark and find ourselves,

For God so loved the world that He gave His one and only Son, that whoever believes in him shall not perish but have eternal life. John 3:16

God loves this world. He loves us. He does not hate us, he loves us. I used to be mad at God. So he created me, he loves me yet I am a sinner and if I don't repent I am going to be thrown into Hell, where I will be eternally tormented. This is what I was taught to believe. Slowly but surely I began to believe the truth. God did not abandon me or us but gave himself. God started all things and God will finish it. Wow! If death came through one man then death was conquered in one man and I am not left alone but I am loved. If I believe this to be true then I already have everlasting life.

Therefore, just as sin entered the world through one man, and death through sin, and in this way death came to all people, because all sinned— Romans 5:12

But the gift is not like the trespass. For if the many died by the trespass of the one man, how much more did God's grace and the gift that came by the grace of the one man, Jesus Christ, overflow to the many! Romans 5:15

The gospel really is good news! We are supposed to experience it, feel it, and know it to be good. I like this quote by Athanasius of Alexandria from On the Incarnation, "It was unworthy of the goodness of God that creatures made by him should be brought to nothing through the deceit wrought upon man by the devil; and it was supremely unfitting that the work of God in mankind should disappear, either through their own negligence or through the deceit of evil spirits."[5]

[5]"Digital Books: On the Incarnation." Blue Letter Bible. Web. 23 Apr, 2020.

<https://www.blueletterbible.org/products/ontheincarnation/index.cfm>.

This book is some of my 25-year journey with God. I want to dedicate it to all who struggle to believe that God is good, to those who have been wounded and traumatised by religion and to the next generation. I love you! You are worthy! I want you to know there is a purpose for your life and a God who loves you.

Introduction

CHAPTER 1

Eternity in the heart

H*e has made everything beautiful in its time. He has also set eternity in the human heart; yet no one can fathom what God has done from beginning to end. Ecclesiastes 3:11*

I looked up at the black night sky. The stars twinkled at me.

"You don't like this very much God do you?" I was addressing God for the first time in a few years. It was a Saturday night in spring. I was 17 years old and at a party. Some of my friends were spewing after too much alcohol, or having a crying fit or rolling in the grass with some boy they didn't really know. The party night had turned sour. What began as "I am free and can do whatever I want" had some not-so-pleasant consequences. I had deliberately chosen to exercise my freedom and had abandoned the "good girl" rules, all rules except sex. This I kept for myself, I did not trust people. Something about the open expanse of sky that night drew me up and I cannot explain it but somehow my thoughts turned to God and what he thought.

I had always been a "deep" child, questioning everything and wanting to know the purpose and point of things. What was the point of the partying? It had only been a few months and it had already lost its shine for me. True, we didn't go to clubs because we were not legally able to do so but we had the alcohol and for some, the drugs. In fact, I distinctly remember being asked at high school if I was a Christian and I answered,

"Well I'm supposed to be but I'm a hypocrite."

I wasn't fooling myself and I didn't want others to call me out. I called myself out. I desperately wished then that I was in a "normal" family. One that wasn't religious. It was limiting to follow the rules. Mind you I swore the most out of my friends and I exercised my liberty, except in the presence of my parents. It was them I hid myself from. I liked the image they had of me, their good, clever girl. There is one who sees though and he saw me on that spring night.

We love because he first loved us. 1John 4:19

He remembered the cry of the eleven-year-old who had prayed, "God if I ever leave you, bring me back to you." I had literally cried one night in bed, feeling this overwhelming burden. I didn't believe at that time that I would go away from God, I had a strong child's faith. I had asked Jesus 'into my heart' at seven. I read my bible and went to church with my parents and I had a love for people, my empathetic gift has always been strong.

There comes a point though when we must leave our parents and find our own way. This is true in all aspects of our lives. As we leave our parent's house naturally so too we must leave our parents "house" of beliefs, thoughts and ideologies. This is good. This is what it takes for each of us to walk in maturity. To question and deconstruct what we have been taught is healthy and necessary.

Eternity was set in my heart. No person if they are honest with themselves wants to cease existing. They may say they will return to dust and that's it. However, if they could choose, who wouldn't choose immortality, especially if it came without conditions. There is something in the human heart that desires everlasting life. Why do we value and idolise youthfulness, can I suggest that it is a picture of life immortal? No youth thinks of their death except if they are suicidal which is a different matter. Older people want to be younger, one day further away from death, age reminds us of our mortality.

There has been in the last decade a massive interest in the supernatural, movies, books, TV series' centre around supernatural creatures, powers and ability. Think of: Twilight, Harry Potter, the Avengers, the Marvel world etc. We are drawn to these things. Why? Because we were created in the image of God whose eternal powers and limitlessness are not comprehended by our current state. We were made though in this image, that the supernatural is more familiar to us than what we consciously remember.

For he chose us in him before the creation of the world to be holy and blameless in his sight. In love he predestined us for adoption to sonship through Jesus Christ, in accordance with his pleasure and will. Ephesians 1:4-5

He chose us before the creation of the world. Somehow we existed before the world was made, in what form exactly I don't know, but we existed in God, we were birthed from her. Finding our way back to God is finding our way home. There are so many verses in scripture describing how carefully crafted we are. One of my favourites is this,

From one man he made all the nations, that they should inhabit the whole earth; and he marked out their appointed times in history and the boundaries of their lands. God did this so that they would seek him and perhaps reach out for him and find him, though he is not far from any one of us. 'For in him we live and move and have our being.' As some of your own poets have said, 'We are his offspring.' Acts 17:26-28

He placed us where we were so we would seek him and perhaps reach out for him. This is what I did again that spring night. I reached out. The restlessness in me was not comforted by my partying. I began to remember, I began to remember where home was.

CHAPTER 2

The wrestle begins

Quite honestly I wasn't and still am not impressed with religion. People fight over it and murder each other. We hide beyond it when we are afraid and excuse bad behaviour based on religious duty. In religion, structures become more important than people. And worse, in my experience at that time; religion was boring. A Sunday church service went something like this; put on my nice Sunday clothes, go to a cold building, sit in rows with odd people and sing some songs, listen to someone talk about something not relevant to my life and the best part, drink coffee and eat biscuits at the end of the meeting. This was of course my subjective experience as a teenager in a Baptist church. There were two exceptions to this, the time the pastor's wife got out of her wheelchair miraculously and which I wasn't there for since the children were in another building. And the Sunday a visiting Evangelist came and said,

"Well ain't those some fancy cars out there in the driveway." My father tells me he still remembers me, on hearing this sitting straight up in my seat and listening to what the guy had to say rather than slouching in my chair with a bored expression on my face picking split ends out of my hair. The visiting Evangelist was not invited back.

One vivid memory I have in Sunday school at around twelve years of age was a lesson concerning Peter walking on the water towards Jesus. I distinctly remember thinking, I don't just want to read stories in the bible I want to experience them. My young mind was beginning to question God's reality. If he was real then I wanted to experience him. I wanted him to speak to me. I wanted to see things I read about happen for me. I am not a person who conforms, I always need to know "why". In school, at home and in the church it was the same, I didn't follow structures because that's what we do, I wanted to know why we do what we do?

I guess that's why I drifted from God at that time, he wasn't real to me. What I had was a list of rules I should follow to be "holy". As a young person experiencing the sudden flood of hormones, these were more real. My self-esteem at this time plummeted. As a perfectionist, I didn't measure up to my own expectations and the expectations I felt projected onto me by the wider society. One example of this is when the boy I liked told me I couldn't sing or made some kind of discouraging remark about my singing. I lost my confidence that day, after always enjoying my voice and singing, I no longer enjoyed it. The power of shame took hold. To this day I don't remember the exact words but I remember the feeling I experienced. When we look to others to be affirmed we give them power over us. Of course, as a pre-teen you don't think about these things, you just experience them. From a young age, I have sought intimacy and connection. My value system for self at that time was built on others to whom I felt connected. Examples included family, authority figures, friends and obviously even at this young age, love interests. I didn't tell anyone of my shame in this situation and it remained for many years. Of course, not all people are so sensitive but I am one of those highly sensitive people scoring almost maximum on the tests.

It is here I want to say something important. In my opinion, there has been an extreme amount of damage done by spirituality that separates the spirit from the other parts of our humanity. We are holistic beings with a body, mind, emotions and will. No one aspect is more sacred than the other. When we repress something it will turn around and bite us. This topic deserves a whole chapter and we will get to that later.

So as a teenager who is transitioning towards adulthood with a flood of new thoughts, feelings and experiences, this is a brave new world and it is exciting. Sitting in a church service with no experiential or emotional sensations towards the people there or God is a real turn-off. It is more fun out there in the 'real' world.

Looking back a series of divine interventions actually got me back in a church service. It was a Friday night and I wanted to go to an all night youth group meeting. It was a stay awake all night and hang-out event. All three of the girls who had promised to come with me canceled at the last minute. Stubborn as I am, I decided I would go by myself. Not ideal for a young person but what could you do? I was a rather independent person, not the group-following kind so going alone, although a bit strange was not a disaster.

At some point in the later stages of the evening, I began talking to a guy who I discovered had a car. "Let's go buy some chocolate!" I not so much asked but demanded. I happily got into a strange guy's car and got driven around with booming music and chocolate. This guy invited me to his church this coming Sunday. It happened to be in the suburb over from my house and because I wasn't one to forsake an adventure, I found myself sitting in a Salvation Army church service ten o'clock Sunday morning by my own choice after not going to church at all for some time.

I will never forget that morning. As I walked through the front doors of the building, standing at the entrance was Jesus. Well he looked like Jesus, there was a light shining all around his head and he had long brown hair. He introduced himself and I was speechless (for once). I stammered something about needing to go brush my hair and rushed off to the bathroom. At the time of writing, I shared this memory with my husband and I found myself saying,

"Isn't that exactly how we are with God. In his presence, we get self-conscious and worry about our mess and want to fix it."

The presence of Jesus in that young man shocked me. It was more intense during the service as I saw this same guy, jump up and down, lay on the ground and worship with a freedom and passion I had never seen before. I was intrigued. The services themselves were quite familiar in the general structure but there was something else. This something else drew me back the next week and the week after that and the weeks following. One morning the pastor gave an altar call, this is where you go up the front if you want to give your life to Jesus. God had been working on me and I felt the nudge. I gripped the chair, There's no way I'm going up, I thought to myself. I'm not giving my whole life to God. What if he sends me to Africa and I die on a foreign mission field somewhere?

No way, I can't. God was not a nice being, he made you do horrible things, uncomfortable things and you had to die. Now understand this, I am a stubborn person but God is more stubborn. I don't know how but I found myself at the front. I gritted my teeth,

"Fine God, you can have my life, I'll stop drinking. (alcohol)"

A few weeks later I was back to my old habits, except now I had shame and condemnation added to that after failing God. (Or rather my own will. I prided myself on having a strong will) This was a difficult time as I struggled to understand what was going on. I had found friends in the church so I didn't want to leave them and I had a huge crush on "Jesus" the shiny light, long-haired guy.

One summer Sunday evening during a service in the church, there was another altar call. I still remember what I was wearing, a striped retro dress and hat. I sat on the carpet and waited. An older man in the church bent down to pray for me. He took off my hat while looking deeply into my eyes, his eyes were piercing blue, fierce and kind. He told me my sins were forgiven and there was no shame or condemnation. I still remember the sensation I felt after he did that. It was as though a rush of wind came and lifted a weight off my shoulders I didn't realise I was carrying. I began to cry, deep sobs. I wasn't the crying sort so this was unusual, a releasing and refreshing feeling came over me. I saw the cross, Jesus took my sin. It became personal. After I had finished crying, this great joy came, I danced, I sang, and I was free. I looked like the "Jesus" guy.

Looking back, I can say it was freedom I was drawn to. After I got home that night, I opened my bible and it flipped to Galatians,

It is for freedom that Christ has set us free. Stand firm, then, and do not let yourselves be burdened again by a yoke of slavery. Galatians 5:1

We are truly meant to be free. This is the call. God is calling out,

"Be free, come out of hiding, I don't mind your mess. It's my job to take hold of you, you don't take hold of yourself.

Not that I have already obtained all this, or have already been made perfect, but I press on to take hold of that for which Christ Jesus took hold of me. Philippians 3:12

Jesus takes hold of us. We don't take hold of him. Yet so much of religious activity is us trying to get to him when if we have accepted his invitation, he has already taken hold of us. The next season of my life is this story, me trying to get hold of Jesus.

CHAPTER 3

Eyes open

Jesus took hold of me in the summer holidays before my last year of high school. All of the people pleasing in me transferred to God. I never would have admitted my people-pleasing ways. I thought I lived in the "I don't care what people think of my zone." At that time in the late '90s, grunge was a huge cultural trend. I embraced it fully, loving my "unique" appearance. (Along with all the other artistic teenagers, we were unique together.)

However, it was a front because inside there was a huge amount of self-hatred and insecurity. Everything from that point on was about God. School didn't mean anything to me anymore and my perfectionism shifted to pleasing God. This is not entirely bad in itself, God is looking for whole-heartedness but that's the point, it's not my actions alone he wants; it's my heart, my affections and my emotions.

Above all else, guard your heart, for everything you do flows from it. Proverbs 4:23

I can tell you, I started doing a lot of stuff. I fasted every prayer meeting day, once a week. (After the meeting I would gobble some takeaway fried chicken, very healthy.) I went to every church meeting and when I joined the worship group, band practice too. I felt I didn't fit into "normal" life anymore, especially school life. I still had my friends and although I didn't 'preach' to them I felt there was a great divide between us. A few of my friends followed me to some church stuff, which helped but since I wasn't partying in the same way anymore, some connections faded away entirely. I still am in some sort of contact with my best friends from high school, true relationship should remain even when we have differing beliefs. However, any feeling of rejection I experienced or loneliness I felt in this season I attributed to "Having taken up my cross to follow Jesus and we must die to ourselves and this hurts". There is truth in this and we will get to that but not all pain comes solely from "the denying of self". In this young stage of my life, I lived in extremes. All things were black and white, grey did not exist.

Age has tempered my tendency to live in extremes, however, I am a passionate person by nature and God knows this and understands. I'm sure he appreciated my grand efforts to please him. Perhaps for him though it must have felt like a bridegroom watching his bride-to-be spend all her time planning for the wedding and doing everything to organise it, while at the same time ignoring the bridegroom who is right there with her.

So there I am full of young zeal and ready to go die for Jesus. I took my faith seriously. I would not be a wishy-washy Jesus follower, I would be a hard-core one. I forgot to mention something and it comes to mind as I write. One time before God interrupted me in my teenage rebellion I remember walking in the city, a street preacher stood on the pavement. Do you know what I did? I felt so embarrassed and ashamed I crossed the road to the other side and looked the other way. I couldn't stand it. Now I was one of those, except I didn't street preach...yet.

I had wanted to study law after high school but it was one of the first things God spoke to me about, "It isn't for you." I felt he said. OK, next I auditioned for a Christian performing arts school.

Do you remember the guy who drove me in his car to buy chocolate? Well we formed a band and wrote songs together and he came to accompany me at my audition, it was for drama and singing. To my shock and delight, I got into the school. Amidst the excitement though, I couldn't shake an uneasy feeling. I asked my prayer group to pray over the decision with me. They felt that it wasn't right for me to attend the school. How could this be? I was devastated. Not even a Christian school was good enough? I lost my energy to figure out what I was going to do and so there I was heading into my

19th year unemployed and at a loss as to know what to do. My Dad didn't understand. (Although he supported me in the midst of it.) He kept telling me how talented I was, so what was I doing? Other kind adults also tried to help me make some choices but I was a deflated balloon.

Nothing helped to lift me up. I applied to study counseling but I wasn't old enough. I tried to find work. It didn't prove to be easy without much experience or qualifications and I began to question my decision making. Was I imagining God? Was I afraid to do something? What was wrong with me? I was afraid of one thing, I was afraid of displeasing God.

I moved out of home and lived with other single people and since I didn't work full-time I had a lot of free time. At the start of the year 1999 I started a prayer journal and every day I would write in it. As the year progressed, my desperation grew,

"God, what are you doing with me? I will go God if you want me to go. I'm yours."

Then Jesus came to them and said, "All authority in heaven and on earth has been given to me. Therefore go and make disciples of all nations, baptizing them in the name of the Father and of the Son and of the Holy Spirit, and teaching them to obey everything I have commanded you. And surely I am with you always, to the very end of the age." Mathew 20:18-20

Everything in me wanted to please God. My heart is still this. To this day I surrender my will to his. Yet at the young age of nineteen with no serious disappointment in life, to give up your dreams, your own desires and your will is a massive thing. There was one thing I started to yearn for in the midst of this struggle; to hear his voice clearly, to KNOW it was him, not to hope it was or not to have to rely on others to hear for me. It is not a bad thing to rely on others, especially when we are a 'baby'. However true growth means I genuinely become less dependent on people and more dependent on God. Ultimately, we need to become interdependent on people and solely dependent on God.

My will was in the bending process and it hurt. I am not going to lie, it was painful. I did receive encouragement along the way. At that time, I visited all kinds of churches and services, I was hungry for spiritual things. People began to pick me out of the crowd and give me words of encouragement, God saw me. I needed this affirmation, for him to single me out in a room full of people meant everything to me. My Mum encouraged me, she gave me this scripture,

Do not conform to the pattern of this world, but be transformed by the renewing of your mind. Then you will be able to test and approve what God's will is—his good, pleasing and perfect will. Romans 12:2

It was at this time I felt God speaking to me specifically from a part in the story of Moses and the Israelites,

Moses said to the people, "Do not be afraid. God has come to test you, so that the fear of God will be with you to keep you from sinning." Exodus 20:20

To sin means to "miss the mark" Was God trying to tell me the fear I had of him (my intense desire to please him) meant I could better understand and know what his will was and not miss the mark?

I remember my affliction and my wandering, the bitterness and the gall. I well remember them, and my soul is downcast within me. Yet this I call to mind and therefore I have hope: Because of the LORD's great love we are not consumed, for his compassions never fail. They are new every morning; great is your faithfulness. The LORD is good to those whose hope is in him, to the one who seeks him; it is good to wait quietly for the salvation of the LORD. It is good for a man to bear the yoke while he is young. Let him sit alone in silence, for the LORD has laid it on him. Let him bury his face in the dust— there may yet be hope. Lamentations 3:19-29

In my distress, the above verses comforted me. They felt very specific to my situation. I was waiting for God, I was young, I was alone and I truly felt like my face was in the dust. While most of my friends were going forward with their lives, whether they were working or studying, partying and dating, I was sitting alone in silence hoping like anything that it wasn't in vain and I wasn't some delusional zealot who had lost sense of reality.

During this time, I began to worship. For me, this meant intentionally going to my room, shutting the door, and turning on Christian music. It helped me shift my focus away from myself and onto God. One afternoon as I was alone in the house and dancing in the living room, something strange happened. I found myself staring down a black hole and feeling as though people were falling into the darkness, on my knees I cried out, I groaned and it was as though the groans came up and out from the depths of my belly. My rational brain was thinking, What on earth is going on right now? While simultaneously feeling pain and emotional agony as I saw this black hole beneath me.

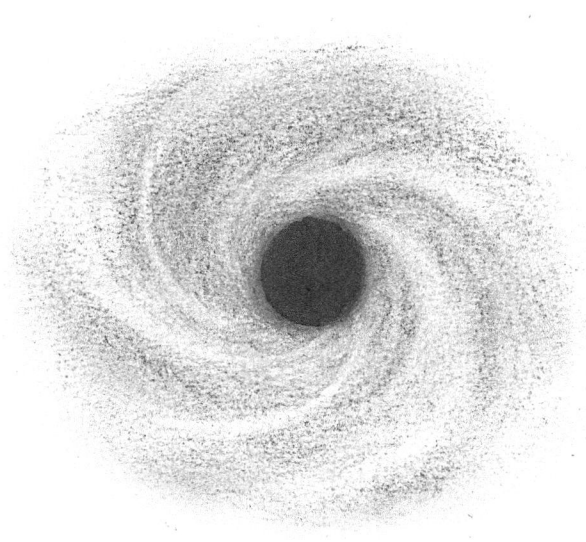

In the same way, the Spirit helps us in our weakness. We do not know what we ought to pray for, but the Spirit himself intercedes for us through wordless groans. And he who searches our hearts knows the mind of the Spirit, because the Spirit intercedes for God's people in accordance with the will of God. Romans 8:26-27

This was my first encounter with the Holy Spirit in this way. I didn't pray in tongues (a spiritual language) at this point, yet this groaning was also a spiritual language. I believe I was feeling God's heart for those who didn't know him and who were heading down the path of death. This experience was shocking and satisfying. To go beyond oneself and enter into the mind of the Spirit-filled my hunger and left me wanting more. This definitely wrought a transformation in me. One moment in the Spirit gave me more understanding about what God wanted than reading ten books on the subject from cover to cover.

I became determined to "hear" God and I set myself to this task one crisp day in September of 1999. I told God,

"I am not leaving my bedroom or eating until you speak to me." This sounds intense and to some unwise, however, I was not interested in what was reasonable I wanted something real. Now I am a person who gets bored easily so to stay in a room without distracting myself with eating and entertainment was taxing. I sat, I waited, I had no clue how this worked. Now you might say I shouldn't be demanding anything from God, and to an extent I agree but there was purity in my desire, I wanted him. I was prepared to wait for as long as it took, God knew my determination. I didn't have to wait longer than half a day. Two words sounded in my mind. They were not physically audible on the outside but they were audible in my mind,

"Isaiah 61." *I'm just making it up I thought to myself, I'm pulling something random from thin air, it's just my imagination.* I was scared to look it up and be disappointed in what it said and it was from the Old Testament section of the bible: Isaiah? I didn't even know what half of all that meant. However the longer I sat there the greater the pressure became, I HAD to look it up,

The Spirit of the Sovereign LORD is on me, because the LORD has anointed me to proclaim good news to the poor. He has sent me to bind up the brokenhearted, to proclaim freedom for the captives and release from darkness for the prisoners, to proclaim the year of the LORD's favor and the day of vengeance of our God, to comfort all who mourn, and provide for those who grieve in Zion— to bestow on them a crown of beauty instead of ashes, the oil of joy instead of mourning, and a garment of praise instead of a spirit of despair. They will be called oaks of righteousness, a planting of the LORD for the display of his splendor. Isaiah 61:1-3

I threw my bible across the room in sheer shock at what it said. I couldn't believe it, it was the secret longing of my heart written in perfect detail. I read it over and over again, crying.

If we follow Christ we all have this anointing. Anointing literally means we are covered or smeared in something, it drips over us and flows out of us and in a spiritual sense, it is given to us by God to be given to others. This is the anointing of Jesus. He read it out in the synagogue and said the prophecy was fulfilled, he was speaking of himself.[6]

For me in this moment it became personal. God's Spirit was on me to release goodness to others. I had asked him to speak to me and he did. I had no prior knowledge of that scripture in Isaiah. My heart was full and I only became more hungry to have God speak to me. God was and is exciting!

An exceptional period in my life started. This was a turning point. Through a series of divinely appointed events by the middle of the next year I was attending a five-month course at a bible college. This was driven by God. Shortly after my Isaiah 61 experience, one of my best friend's attending university in another city asked me to visit her. On a Sunday evening, we spontaneously decided to visit a church service. We arrived as the last person there was locking the building. He suggested we go to a certain cafe where some of the young adults had planned to go.

[6] Luke 4:14-30

We went, we knew nobody. I ended up sitting opposite a guy who told me about a course he had just been on and the exciting supernatural things he had experienced there. My heart burned within me and I knew I had to go to the same school.

I had no money but I said to God,

"If you want me to go you will have to provide because I'm not going into debt for it." Shortly after I got a phone call from my ex-boyfriend asking me if I wanted to go to a job interview. I got that job and it was a five-minute bicycle ride from my house. Think of the odds, I was not in my ex's favour but I was with God! I had tried to find a job all that year and then suddenly I got one without me having to do anything, that was not a coincidence. I worked for six months to save for my course which was only half the amount needed, the weekly student allowance paid for the rest.

The course was five months and it was named, Certificate in Evangelism. There was a focus on living by faith. I thought I was going to go there to do something for God. Little did I know it would all be about what he wanted to do/be for me. I am sharing quite a lot about the early days because it lays a foundation for where I want us to get to. There would be so many stories I could share from my over twenty-five-year relationships with God but the early ones are important because everything else I have learned has been built upon them.

The school was a fun time for me; meeting new people and living on campus in a secluded but beautiful coastal area in New Zealand. Finally, my life was moving forward. There was one aspect of the course I found difficult, the street evangelism part. For me to go on the streets of the biggest city in New Zealand and try to evangelise to random people was terrible. I am not a confrontational person and I easily sense other people's emotions. One time before I attended school my youth pastor asked me to street preach. The crowd was tiny, only six to ten people besides our youth team.

I remember taking the microphone with trembling hands, I began by sharing how much God loves people and I could not control the wave of pain that came over me, half of my preaching time I just stood there and cried. I was not eloquent or doing a good job in apologetics (reasoned arguments to justify the Christian faith), instead, I wept as I felt God's heart of love.

So imagine me on the streets, I felt useless. The teaching in the school was excellent in terms of love. The motivation on the streets was to love people. We were encouraged to see everybody as "pre-Christian" or Christian and to move all one step closer in their relationship with God. One evening I simply handed out flowers as a love offering from God to the recipient. But still, I struggled. Every time we went, I felt as though I failed. I didn't "see" any results.

It is easy to understand my process looking back but at the time I had no understanding of the bigger picture and what God was doing. A few weeks in on the course I had gone to my room to pray and intercede, my journal entry describing this reads,

"*Many doubts, hurt, an intense longing to please the Lord. I want to be free of cynicism and pride. I sobbed to the Lord. I grew extremely weary and curled up on my bed. I saw a picture of his hand stroking my face, as a father to a child, a truly beautiful spiritual moment. I fell asleep for about half an hour and when I woke up I was 'still' inside, peaceful. This psalm came to mind. The Lord had forced me to be still, he stilled my spirit.*"

My heart is not proud, LORD, my eyes are not haughty; I do not concern myself with great matters or things too wonderful for me. But I have calmed and quieted myself, I am like a weaned[7] child with its mother; like a weaned child I am content. Israel, put your hope in the LORD both now and forevermore. Psalm 131

I had gone to my room to be a warrior, to be disciplined and put on my army boots but I ended up sleeping like a baby. The peace afterward was amazing.

---

[7] A weaned child in this context is about three years old.

For the kingdom of God is not a matter of eating and drinking, but of righteousness, <u>peace</u>[8] and joy in the Holy Spirit. Romans 4:17

You would think I would have learned something from this experience, but no, not yet. What was to come was one of the biggest unravellings of my mind: we can call this a stronghold, a set way of thinking. This stronghold was going to take years to be entirely demolished. It is difficult to sum up what it is exactly but I call it this, 'religion-what I must do to please God'. I want to please God, even as I write I want to sense his pleasure for me but like most things, it is all about our motivation. My religious sense of duty was based on earning God's approval. Some people once asked Jesus about this after he had talked about working for God,

Do not work for food that spoils, but for food that endures to eternal life, which the Son of Man will give you. For on him God the Father has placed his seal of approval." Then they asked him, "What must we do to do the works God requires?" Jesus answered, "The work of God is this: to <u>believe</u>[9] in the one he has sent." John 6:27-29

Did you notice what Jesus said, the work of God is to believe. In the greek this word is pisteuó and means: to believe, commit to and trust in. It is a relational word. It is not a doing word. My mindset was stuck in a "doing" mentality in regard to my relationship with God, including my desire to please him. Even my pastor at the Salvation Army church had said to me earlier that year,

"Jenna you are not chasing a shadow. Jesus is living he wants your heart."

I didn't know it then but my heart was stuck. It was buried inside me. One of my bible lecturers had said to me the day after my weaned child experience that I must choose to walk with my whānau[10] and that I was safe at the college and was with people I could trust. I did have an issue trusting anyone or anything and this was about to change.

[8] Underlined for emphasis
[9] Underlined for emphasis
[10] Whānau is the Māori word for family, I would like to add in some New Zealand culture since it is part of my roots.

Five days during our course time had been set apart for a special topic. An outside lecturer was called in. The week's theme is The Father Heart of God. I wasn't expecting anything much from this week but from the first moment it began my chest tightened and I wondered what I had stumbled into. Our teacher was a gloriously joyful pastor, who actually pastored a church in my home city. From the moment he opened his mouth I couldn't put the pieces together, who was he talking about? The defining moment came, he said,

"Close your eyes. Now picture Father God. What does he look like? Where are you? Can you go near to Father God? What does he do when you come near?" I saw a great throne with someone sitting on it, a blurred, huge, mainly white figure. No way could I go near that throne, it was too holy, too huge. I was afraid. I was not going near it, that was for sure. The pastor explained that what we see may explain how we view God or more precisely our Father God. I began to realise something. I never prayed to Father or used that as a title for God. I used Lord, Jesus, God, Holy Spirit but not the Father. Father God, I saw as distant and demanding with a stick in His hand ready to strike me down if I did something wrong.

The next few days I was introduced to some revolutionary concepts for me. The first one to cause my head to turn upside down was this one,

Moreover, the Father judges no one, but has entrusted all judgment to the Son. John 5:22 What did this mean? It means exactly what it reads, all judgement has been passed to Jesus. So is Jesus judging me now?

Who then is the one who condemns? No one. Christ Jesus who died—more than that, who was raised to life—is at the right hand of God and is also interceding for us. Romans 8:34 No!

According to this scripture, Jesus is at God's right hand and is interceding for us. Well, what about the Holy Spirit then? He must be condemning us and sorting out our unholiness,

In the same way, the Spirit helps us in our <u>weakness</u>[11]. We do not know what we ought to pray for, but the Spirit himself intercedes for us through wordless groans. Romans 8:26 No, the Spirit is helping us. Is God not condemning us at all then? No! Neither the Father, the Son, or the Holy Spirit are condemning us.

Therefore, there is now no condemnation for those who are in Christ Jesus. Romans 8:1

Why did we go from judgement to condemnation? It seems we equate these two actions as the same thing. They are not. The dictionary[12] defines judgement as this:the process of forming an opinion or evaluation by discerning and comparing and the capacity for judgement:discernment. Judgement also means, a formal utterance of an authoritative opinion and a formal decision given by a court and the final judging of humankind by God, a divine sentence or decision specifically:a calamity held to be sent by God.

We attribute to God mainly the second two definitions and skip entirely the first one. Wouldn't you like to have someone to have a balanced and discerning viewpoint in regard to you and your actions. I would, especially if that viewpoint is from someone who sees perfectly and knows everything. From what I understood of myself I believe I was also confusing judgement and condemnation, meaning when I heard the word judgement I was unconsciously feeling condemned. How does the dictionary[13] define condemned? Declared to be reprehensible, wrong, or evil, pronounced guilty and sentenced to punishment, officially declared to be unfit for use.

Can you see how we confuse these two words even the word "judgement" itself conjures up the idea of disapproval and punishment which is a condemnation, not judgement.

---

[11] Underlined for emphasis
[12] https://www.merriam-webster.com/dictionary/judgement
[13] https://www.merriam-webster.com/dictionary/condemned

Ok so in my mind it was God the Father who judged (or as I wrongly understood "condemned") me. Now I knew all judgement had been passed to Jesus I had no reason to stand back at a distance.

Jesus said,

No, the Father himself loves you because you have loved me and have believed that I came from God. John 16:27

Now this is eternal life: that they know[14] you, the only true God, and Jesus Christ, whom you have sent. John 17:3

The Father himself loves us and we have eternal life when we KNOW God and Jesus Christ. This word **know** in greek is ginōskō. This word means; to learn, to know, come to know, get a knowledge of perceive, feel. The word has included within its meaning to know via the five senses and 'to know' someone was a Jewish idiom for sexual intimacy.

How intimately does God want to know us? You might say, well if God knows everything, she knows us already. Yes but just as Christ limited himself in a human body so does God limit herself in the knowledge of us in terms of intimacy. Forced intimacy is abuse. I am getting ahead of myself.

In that Fatherheart God week, I encountered God in a whole new way. Not only had my mindset in relation to him been wrong but my own physical illness as a child and the physical illnesses of my earthly father resulted in a sense of loss and unhealthy independence which projected itself onto my relationship with God. Our parents are images of God to us and when those images crack, break or are nonexistent this reflects in our relationship with the Parent of us all-God. This is a huge topic and many wonderful books have been written on this subject.

In my encounter with God, I saw him step down from his throne, walk over to where I was, pick me up and put me on his knee. I wrote this poem to illustrate that experience. I named it Daddy.

[14] Underlined for emphasis

Many mindsets, confusion, judgement, striving, dead.

The Father judges no-one.

The Son judges, the price is paid. Innocence is proclaimed.

Freedom reigns Intimacy is pivotal. Let us walk together.

You stood.

Looked at me,

And walked down from your throne. You came to me

And with a soft sound,

Mouth quivering, shy and joyfully expectant I said, "Hi Lord"

And with that I laid my head on your shoulder. We sat in companionable silence.

Breathing in beauty and peace.

My heart beat with a thousand words of contentment. Words of love

Words of praise

I lifted my head from your shoulder, Looked full in your face,

"Here I am",

Was all I needed to say before again we lapsed into a knowing silence.

The cobwebs are cleared from my mind, clarity, forgiveness, rest, fulfillment, truth, life. Revelation penetrates the darkest depths of my soul.

From my innermost being I see a lost, lonely little girl who longs for her Daddy. To be Daddy's little girl.

To be comforted, hugged and kissed. To hear sweet endearments.

To feel safe, warm, secure and loved.

Circumstances blow my dream apart.

Poverty and sickness of spirit and mind shatter my home. Peace and rest fly out the window.

Hope is but a mere feather, Small and insignificant, Fluttering at the window pane

Strain and pain rear their ugly faces.

Tiny intimate moments are snatched away all too soon.

Injustice becomes a reality "Why" the all-consuming question.

Fences are built.

The heart is fortified.

Forced strength and an almost appropriate apathy become a girl's best friend. Masks are worn.

The path becomes laborious. Life must go on.

Love struggles and still we go on. The foundation of hardness is laid. We can cope.

We have courage.

And the little girl is left crouching behind those closed walls.

Until the day her heavenly Father lifts the roof off her fortress and exposes the forgotten child. Tear streaked cheeks are lifted up to heaven.

The wound is bared to herself.

The Father plucks the little girl out of her hole and places her in His arms. Stroking her and soothing her fears.

He understands. Condemnation is no more.

Healing has begun.

Jesus came to show us what God is like. He came to show us our Father.

Philip said, "Lord, show us the Father and that will be enough for us." Jesus answered: "Don't you know me, Philip, even after I have been among you such a long time? Anyone who has seen me has seen the Father. How can you say, 'Show us the Father'? Don't you believe that I am in the Father, and that the Father is in me? The words I say to you I do not speak on my own authority. Rather, it is the Father, living in me, who is doing his work. John 14:8-10

"You heard me say, 'I am going away and I am coming back to you.' If you loved me, you would be glad that I am going to the Father, for the Father is greater than I. John 14:28

James Jordan writes in his book *Sonship a Journey into Father's heart* that "Jesus is not the doorway to **get to** heaven. ***He is the door for the Father to come to us!***"[15]

The Father came to me. This changed everything.

---

[15] From Sonship a Journey into Father's heart. By James Jordan © 2012 Fatherheart Media

CHAPTER 4

Religion burns out

A few other significant things happened while I was at bible school. During deliverance week I got free from the shame I had received after I had believed the words of the boy who had said I couldn't sing. I was being prayed for by a woman leader and I saw a black wall in front of me. The leader sensed it too and she asked me,

"Jenna, what is that?" I replied I didn't know and after a while, she discerned it was shame.

She told the shame to leave my voice and I literally felt that wall come down. Secondly, my spiritual eyes were opened and I began to see spirits, good ones and bad ones.

My spiritual sight had opened during our outreach time, in fact, one of the leaders at school had prophesied to me before going that,

"Outreach would be significant for me, God is going to speak and uncover what has been hidden from me." We had some bizarre experiences during that outreach and there was an instance of my co-leader and I (I had been made co-leader with my friend for our team) seeing the exact same spirit. We described its appearance to each other as we saw it in the moment. This confirmed that what I saw wasn't only in my imagination which could be likely since I'm an imaginative person.

Unfortunately, the bad ones seemed to be more abundant than the good ones and it was disconcerting. I remember the day a few girls in our dormitory gathered us together and wanted to go through the whole dorm and pray in every room. We were very good crusaders, and off we went.

The further down the hallway we went, the worse we felt. We arrived at the last bedroom. Those at the front stopped short. One girl in the front started gagging and the others refused to go in. What on earth was in there? I marched in. Black figures and ugly-looking creatures covered the perimeter of the room. It's hard to explain how spiritual sight works. I could see the figures there but they were not there in a material form. Fear came over me, I had to get out. However, something else rose up within me, some kind of holy anger. How dare these demons threaten us or invade our building

(It hadn't been particularly nice to shovel toilet sewage earlier in the week, there had been other problems in our dormitory also which we attributed to demonic influence). I opened my mouth to yell and a fierce foreign language came out. (This was my first experience of speaking in tongues boldly, a phenomenon mentioned in scripture after the disciples were baptised by the Holy Spirit[16])

I watched as the room emptied of those nasty harassers. Later that evening in the lounge of our dormitory I saw huge angels stationed at the four corners of the room, they towered above the building. I pondered what I was seeing. It was a weird world all these spiritual beings, what had I stepped into? What would happen when I left bible school? This may sound strange but when I looked at the campus I felt as though there was a bubble around us, a protective shield like something you would see in a science fiction movie. Anything that happened on campus was allowed by God to train and equip us, so the dormitory "invasion" was only an exercise or war game.

Right before the five months of the course were up I had a breakthrough in street outreach. I was fed up with the whole thing and I stumbled into my breakthrough by giving up. I sat down on the bench and in frustration told God,

---

[16] See Acts 2:1-6

"If you want me to talk to someone you can send them to this bench to sit beside me." Someone did come at some point and that was the most fruitful conversation and connection I had had with anyone up until that time. Are you laughing? It's completely true. To this day I well remember this lesson. All my self-effort produces striving and stress, if I give up my own work I am more likely to see something happen.

'Not by might nor by power, but by my Spirit,' says the Lord Almighty. Zechariah 4:6

This is the crux of the matter. Do you think I remembered this after I left bible college and went home. No, I did not. I went right back to my old mindset. This is the mindset of religion. It is all about what I can do. And it was going to take some time yet before I really did give up.

Going back to my hometown and local church was difficult. I had had all these crazy experiences and now I was going back to the "normal" church routine. What I didn't realize at the time was that I was about to step into the most difficult and necessary experience yet. Being at bible school was like catapulting off the launch pad. My training had only just begun. Added to this I had formed a strong bond with a boy at bible school, he went back to his hometown and I missed him dreadfully. After a few months, Holy Spirit spoke to him that we were to only be friends. (I knew in my heart it was true but I had been ignoring it) He called me in the evening on the day I had written this in my journal,

"I want to be consumed by fire. I want to be a firebrand. I want you Lord, I choose you today, I choose you."

This was bitterly painful and unlocked in me a grief that I couldn't shake. Loneliness became a constant feeling. Every time somebody prayed for me, they would ask God to come to my lonely place and comfort me. One Saturday the feeling was awful. I went to my room to worship and as I stood there with tears streaming down my face, I distinctly heard the voice of my

Father,

"Never will I leave you, never will I forsake you." I heard this repeated over and over and I wept uncontrollably as Holy Spirit spoke those words. In that season I held on to this truth for dear life. I needed God more than ever as I struggled to be obedient to his guidance. It wasn't a sacrifice God wanted, it was my heart. Psalm 40 has always been important to me and has significant meaning in many ways. Verses six to eight say this,

Sacrifice and offering you did not desire— <u>but my ears you have opened</u>[17]— burnt offerings and sin offerings you did not require. Then I said, "Here I am, I have come— it is written about me in the scroll. I desire to do your will, my God; your law is within my heart." Psalm 40:6-8

The underlined section could also be translated from the Hebrew translation, you have pierced my ear and is a reference to a bond servant who in that time and culture pierced their ear as a sign of wanting to serve their master for life. I had asked God to pierce my ear and now he was holding me good on my commitment. Except he did not want what I could sacrifice or offer to him, he wanted my heart and my desire. We can sacrifice something or offer something but if it doesn't come from a place of joy or passion, what kind of offering is that? A dutiful one with no pleasure involved. My journey in knowing God was beginning and in this stage his reality remained at a distance. How long does it take to really know someone? I have been married for twelve years (at the time of writing) and it is only now I can say I am beginning to know my husband. God is a consuming fire,

For the Lord your God is a consuming fire, a jealous God. Deuteronomy 4:24

I had asked him to come burn me and I was feeling it. The fire was burning away the crap and as the year progressed it got worse. I saw demonic beings consistently, this didn't help. I began to have difficulties eating, I experienced anxiety and my fears were amplified.

---

[17] Underlined for emphasis

This and an overwhelming feeling of not doing enough. I felt weak and stressed. There was one day in July of 2001 after going to work (I worked part time in a cafe) as I stood on the side of the road and watched a truck rush past I thought, What if I went under the wheels of the truck, it might be easier than all this."

My suicide thought shocked me. Where the heck was I to be in this situation? In desperation, I cancelled my plans that evening which were to go to youth group and I determined as I had earlier to hear from God. I sat in my living room and waited. I had no other option, I needed an answer. One word came to mind-Bakka. (spelt as I heard it) I had never heard of that. Surely, I was hearing nonsense, but it wouldn't diminish so in doubt I checked my concordance. To my shock, there was one reference matching what I had heard,

How lovely is your dwelling place, LORDAlmighty!My soul yearns, even faints, for the courts of the LORD; my heart and my flesh cry out for the living God. Even the sparrow has found a home, and the swallow a nest for herself, where she may have her young— a place near your altar, LORD Almighty, my King and my God. Blessed are those who dwell in your house; they are ever praising you. Blessed are those whose strength is in you, whose hearts are set on pilgrimage. As they pass through the Valley of Baka, [18] they make it a place of springs; the autumn rains also cover it with pools. They go from strength to strength, till each appears before God in Zion. Psalm 84:1-7

The bible study note said this about the Valley of Baka,

Means either "weeping" or "Balsam trees" The joyful expectations of the pilgrims transforms the difficult ways into places of refreshment...By God's benevolent care over his pilgrims, the vale of weeping (or balsam trees), already transformed by the glad hearts of the expectant wayfarers, is turned into a valley of praise. [19]

[18] Underlined for emphasis
[19] Taken from The NIV Study bible 1985 by the Zondervan corporation

God did not deliver me instantly in that moment out of my distress but he told me where I was and that he was with me. I was in a place of weeping but the promise was that through my expectancy and continued praise it would be transformed into a joyful place. Wow, reading this now almost twenty years later I am amazed at the grace of God. By keeping me in that difficult place he was teaching me how to remain in him no matter the circumstances. My inner self was expanding to be able to handle more. It IS painful. There is no way around it. When we are stretched it hurts.

In your struggle against sin, you have not yet resisted to the point of shedding your blood. And have you completely forgotten this word of encouragement that addresses you as a father addresses his son? It says, "My son, do not make light of the Lord's discipline, and do not lose heart when he rebukes you, because the Lord disciplines the one he loves, and he chastens everyone he accepts as his son. Endure hardship as discipline; God is treating you as his children. For what children are not disciplined by their father? If you are not disciplined—and everyone undergoes discipline—then you are not legitimate, not true sons and daughters at all. Moreover, we have all had human fathers who disciplined us and we respected them for it. How much more should we submit to the Father of spirits and live! They disciplined us for a little while as they thought best; but God disciplines us for our good, in order that we may share in his holiness. No discipline seems pleasant at the time, but painful. Later on, however, it produces a harvest of righteousness and peace for those who have been trained by it. Therefore, strengthen your feeble arms and weak knees. Make level paths for your feet," so that the lame may not be disabled, but rather healed. Hebrews 12:4-13

God was fathering me. If he saved me instantly from everything, how would I learn to do things? My growth would be stunted. That evening I also saw a ring of fire, I felt it was a place being prepared for me. I did not understand what it meant then however I do now, in scripture it says this,

And I myself will be a wall of fire around it,' declares the LORD, 'and I will be its glory within.' Zechariah 2:5

"It" in this instance is Jerusalem, however we are Jerusalem since we are the temple where God lives. There is a wall of fire surrounding us as protection, I had not yet experienced this. I needed to come into this experiential reality and God was leading me to that place. Let's look at this story from scripture,

Now the king of Aram was at war with Israel. After conferring with his officers, he said, "I will set up my camp in such and such a place." The man of God sent word to the king of Israel: "Beware of passing that place, because the Arameans are going down there." So the king of Israel checked on the place indicated by the man of God. Time and again Elisha warned the king, so that he was on his guard in such places. This enraged the king of Aram. He summoned his officers and demanded of them, "Tell me! Which of us is on the side of the king of Israel?" None of us, my lord the king," said one of his officers, "but Elisha, the prophet who is in Israel, tells the king of Israel the very words you speak in your bedroom." Go, find out where he is," the king ordered, "so I can send men and capture him." The report came back: "He is in Dothan. Then he sent horses and chariots and a strong force there. They went by night and surrounded the city. When the servant of the man of God got up and went out early the next morning, an army with horses and chariots had surrounded the city. "Oh no, my lord! What shall we do?" the servant asked. "Don't be afraid," the prophet answered. "Those who are with us are more than those who are with them." And Elisha prayed, "Open his eyes, LORD, so that he may see." Then the LORD opened the servant's eyes, and he looked and saw the hills full of horses and chariots of fire all around Elisha.[20] *As the enemy came down toward him, Elisha prayed to the LORD, "Strike this army with blindness." So he struck them with blindness, as Elisha had asked. 2 Kings 6:8-18*

Elisha was not afraid of the enemy because he saw God's protection around him and his servant and not only that, God blinded the enemy so they couldn't even see Elisha. We need not fear but I feared a lot. A dear prophet friend in my church gave me Psalm 91 in the midst of my struggle. It says,

[20] Underlined for emphasis

Whoever <u>dwells</u>[21] in the shelter of the Most High will <u>rest</u>[22] in the shadow of the Almighty. I will say of the LORD, "He is my refuge and my fortress, my God, in whom I trust." Surely he will save you from the fowler's snare and from the deadly pestilence. He will cover you with his feathers, and under his wings you will find refuge; his faithfulness will be your shield and rampart. You will not fear the terror of night, nor the arrow that flies by day, nor the pestilence that stalks in the darkness, nor the plague that destroys at midday. A thousand may fall at your side, ten thousand at your right hand, but it will not come near you. You will only observe with your eyes and see the punishment of the wicked. If you say, "The LORD is my refuge," and you make the Most High your dwelling, no harm will overtake you, no disaster will come near your tent. For he will command his angels concerning you to guard you in all your ways; they will lift you up in their hands, so that you will not strike your foot against a stone. You will tread on the lion and the cobra; you will trample the great lion and the serpent. "Because he loves me," says the LORD, "I will rescue him; I will protect him, for he acknowledges my name. He will call on me, and I will answer him; I will be with him in trouble, I will deliver him and honor him. With long life I will satisfy him and show him my salvation." Psalm 91

Did you notice what it says? The one who dwells under God will rest. What we are talking about here is transitioning from what some people call spiritual warfare to a place of rest. I had been experiencing this spiritual warfare in bible college and when I went home the intensity increased. I was a great lover of the image of a bride with warrior boots on and although I don't think this image is wrong necessarily, I interpreted certain parts of scripture in my own way or in the way I had been taught. For example the passage below,

Finally, be strong in the Lord and in his mighty power. Put on the full armor of God, so that you can take your stand against the devil's schemes.

---

[21] Underlined for emphasis
[22] Underlined for emphasis

For our struggle is not against flesh and blood, but against the rulers, against the authorities, against the powers of this dark world and against the spiritual forces of evil in the heavenly realms. Therefore put on the full armor of God, so that when the day of evil comes, you may be able to stand your ground, and after you have done everything, to stand. Stand firm then, with the belt of truth buckled around your waist, with the breastplate of righteousness in place, and with your feet fitted with the readiness that comes from the gospel of peace. In addition to all this, take up the shield of faith, with which you can extinguish all the flaming arrows of the evil one. Take the helmet of salvation and the sword of the Spirit, which is the word of God. And pray in the Spirit on all occasions with all kinds of prayers and requests. With this in mind, be alert and always keep on praying for all the Lord's people. Ephesians 6:10-18

We love the idea of being strong and we exalt hero figures and warriors. This is not a bad thing, we all need a superhero. This passage raises up our inner warrior. This is good we are meant to be as warriors. Following patterns and formulas appeals to our sense of order and security. I had been taught to put on my armour every day. I knew some who literally quoted these verses daily and prayed this over themselves. I wanted to do this however I literally didn't have the energy for it. It was at this time a struggle to survive and in the most basic way; go to work, eat sleep and socialise. My journal notes for October of that year say this,

"I rest in you for the first time in ages. My body is restful. I feel almost lazy. Help me Jesus to do the Father's will." Four days later I wrote, "Had a migraine yesterday, stayed in bed all day."

I remember that migraine day, I had been feeling a burden for a co-worker, a particularly difficult person to be around and I had been feeling pressure to "evangelise" to her. I had this constant feeling that I needed to do more for God and people. Everything in me fought the idea of rest.

Soldiers do not rest, they fight.

Ultimately our armour is Christ himself. Jesus said he is the truth, Christ is our righteousness, Christ is our peace, the faith of Jesus is our faith, Christ is our salvation. We often make it all about us, yet it is all about him. He makes it about us as we make it about him, this is the circle of love.

My resources were thin at this time. My living situation was difficult. I felt a certain responsibility towards my flatmates. In November, I got an invitation to live with some others. It was owned by an older lady and the house was beautiful and in a central location, much closer to my work. My room was in the sleep-out so it was separated from the rest of the house where the kitchen, bathroom and living room areas were. The room was painted lavender and I nicknamed it my 'little purple sanctuary'. I was instantly relieved when I arrived here. The beauty and peace comforted me and I enjoyed my friendship with the owner of the house and my other flatmates. Yet the spiritual pressure increased. I would wake up in the night in fear with cold sweats and my eating did not improve. Added to this I took a nap every day, it was a way of escaping.

There was one thing I did though, every morning I would worship with music. Scientific studies show that music activates every area of our brain[23]. This combined with focusing my attention on God rather than myself "saved me" in this season. For those few minutes, I would be elevated above my circumstances and be free from the weight I was under.

By now it is January of 2002. It is the annual Parachute festival[24] in New Zealand and I cannot get off my bedroom floor to go. I went to the doctor's for a check-up but there was nothing physically wrong with me. I was burnt out at the tender age of 21. The pressure of religion had got me.

[23] Science Daily. Academy of Finland Dec. 6th 2011
[24] "Parachute" was one of the largest Christian music festivals held outside of the United States and it was one of the largest multi-day festivals in the Southern hemisphere running from 1992-2014.

CHAPTER 5

God's love burns up

As I lay on the floor that day all my resources spent, no energy left to even be emotional I heard this,

"Jenna, you can do nothing without me."

"I am the vine; you are the branches. If you remain in me and I in you, you will bear much fruit; apart from me you can do nothing." John 15:5

My condition was revealed. I was still trying to do things without God. BUT I CAN DO NOTHING WITHOUT HIM! I wasn't living IN HIM, or in the least I didn't understand the nature of the relationship I was in. To all the lovers out there; come to the greatest lover for it is not your works/ hands he wants but your face, your being, your heart. The bride is being prepared for Jesus. It is a people who know they are one with him. I am getting ahead of myself but oh this divine invitation to a mystical union is pure ecstasy.

My flatmate asked me a few months later,

"Jenna, what's your call? What's everybody's call?" (He was speaking about the calling God has for us.)

"To extend his kingdom" I replied.

"No, to have an intimate relationship with him," he said.

This "works" mentality was so stuck in my brain that even in a physical burnout I still didn't get it. This is how strong this mentality is and it is the basis on which world religions are founded. What do I need to do to appease/ please my god/gods? Atheists, I appreciate you and your choice to not work for a god. It is a heavy burden. And yes God initiated and instituted Judaism. This is the religion Jesus was born into, he said this about it,

"Do not think that I have come to abolish the Law or the Prophets; I have not come to abolish them but to <u>fulfill</u>[25] them. For truly I tell you, until heaven and earth disappear, not the smallest letter, not the least stroke of a pen, will by any means disappear from the Law until everything is <u>accomplished</u>[26].Mathew 5:17-18

Jesus came to fulfill the requirements of the law, the religion. The law would not disappear until everything was accomplished. What was this accomplishing? It was that God became man and died a death so that blood would be given to cover sin (missing the mark) and death would be conquered. I always wondered, Why blood? Why does there need to be blood shed to deal with sin. In Leviticus it says,

For the life of a creature is in the blood, and I have given it to you to make atonement for yourselves on the altar; it is the blood that makes atonement for one's life. Leviticus 17:11

Jesus who is God became flesh,

The Word became flesh and made his dwelling among us. We have seen his glory, the glory of the one and only Son, who came from the Father, full of grace and truth. John 1:14

God then poured his own blood out to cover us and conquered death for us. Death was the consequence of Adam and Eve's bad decision (sin) that left all of humanity burdened with the same consequence. I love God's passion to rescue us as described here in Isaiah,

Who is this coming from Edom, from Bozrah, with his garments stained crimson? Who is this, robed in splendor, striding forward in the greatness of his strength? "It is I, proclaiming victory, mighty to save." Isaiah 63:1

---

[25] Underlined for emphasis
[26] Underlined for emphasis

Then more radically God the Holy Spirit would come and live inside humanity so we could fulfill the law (because we cannot do it ourselves, it is actually God in us who does) which is as Jesus said is,

" *'Love the Lord your God with all your heart and with all your soul and with all your mind. This is the first and greatest commandment. And the second is like it: 'Love your neighbor as yourself.' All the Law and the Prophets hang on these two commandments." Mathew 22:37-40*

The 'law' is to Love God, love others and love self. Paul writes it this way,

You, my brothers and sisters, were called to be free. But do not use your freedom to indulge the flesh[27]; rather, serve one another humbly in love. For the entire law is fulfilled in keeping this one command: "Love your neighbor as yourself." Galatians 5:13-14

Jesus said,

My command is this: Love each other as I have loved you. Greater love has no one than this: to lay down one's life for one's friends. You are my friends if you do what I command. John 15:12- 14

When we sin, we wound either God, others or ourselves. This wounding breaks a relationship. Think of any of the Ten Commandments. If I violate any of them, I will hurt someone else. If I steal, I will hurt my neighbour. If I worship another god, I will hurt God. God's heart for humanity is that we would live in a place where there is no pain, suffering or darkness. The ultimate utopia. It is greater than nirvana. Universal love as an ideal expressed in the new age movement did not originate from there, it originated from the heart of our Father. It is wounding to God to leave her out. God is the source of all love and we were made to live from this place. When we leave God out we are eating once again from the tree of the knowledge of good and evil.

---

[27] In contexts like this, the Greek word for flesh (sarx) refers to the sinful state of human beings, often presented as a power in opposition to the Spirit. Taken from NIV text notes.

As we seek to live in unity and love each other which is noble and good; leaving God out of this picture means grieving the one who made us. Not only this, it means we will die. Death was not a punishment God gave to humanity but a consequence of cutting ourselves off from the source of life. Like a phone that eventually dies when it is not charged.

Scripture begins in a garden and ends in a garden. God will be with us and there will be no more death or pain. Our hope is in this,

Then I saw "a new heaven and a new earth," for the first heaven and the first earth had passed away, and there was no longer any sea. I saw the Holy City, the new Jerusalem, coming down out of heaven from God, prepared as a bride beautifully dressed for her husband. And I heard a loud voice from the throne saying, "Look! God's dwelling place is now among the people, and he will dwell with them. They will be his people, and God himself will be with them and be their God. Revelation 21:1-4

Then the angel showed me the river of the water of life, as clear as crystal, flowing from the throne of God and of the Lamb down the middle of the great street of the city. On each side of the river stood the tree of life, bearing twelve crops of fruit, yielding its fruit every month. And the leaves of the tree are for the healing of the nations. No longer will there be any curse. The throne of God and of the Lamb will be in the city, and his servants will serve him. They will see his face, and his name will be on their foreheads. There will be no more night. They will not need the light of a lamp or the light of the sun, for the Lord God will give them light. And they will reign for ever and ever. Revelation 22:1-5

This is the gospel of the kingdom. Jesus showed us what it looks like when he healed hearts and bodies, as he welcomed all who came to him and wiped away their tears by healing disease, raising the dead and loving the rejected. He was God with us and He is still God with us as Holy Spirit lives in each one of us who come to Jesus.

This beautiful gospel is love. It is a consuming fire and it is not about what I do but a place I live in.

And so we know and rely on the love God has for us. God is love. Whoever lives in love lives in God, and God in them. 1 John 4:16

Jesus said the kingdom was in us,

Once, on being asked by the Pharisees when the kingdom of God would come, Jesus replied, "The coming of the kingdom of God is not something that can be observed, nor will people say, 'Here it is,' or 'There it is,' because the kingdom of God is within you[28]" Luke 17:20-21

The kingdom is God. He is the king. The kingdom is love, for God is love. The kingdom is light. The kingdom is the way, the truth and life. The kingdom is not an external construction it is the very person of Christ and who he is. The kingdom is God with us and there is no darkness, no pain, no grief, no sorrow, no sin; hurting God, another person or yourself. It is perfect in the kingdom. The kingdom of God is greater than the perfect fairytale. You see fairytales tell the truth. We will live happily ever after. Everything you dream about in your heart is a reality if you step inside this kingdom of love.

It is this kingdom that Jesus asked us to go forth with and make disciples of. We are the kingdom. All my efforts to try and build the kingdom were externally oriented. God on the other hand first wanted his kingdom of love to be built on the inside of me as Paul writes,

My dear children, for whom I am again in the pains of childbirth until Christ is formed in you, Galatians 4:19

I was about to reach a great turning point. I began to meditate on love. If God is love then God is everything love is described as being. If we take Paul's famous description of love and place God's name in there we begin to see a clear picture of the character of God.

God is patient, God is kind. He does not envy, he does not boast, he is not proud. He does not dishonor others, he is not self-seeking, he is not easily angered, he keeps no record of wrongs.

[28] Some translations say "in your midst" but the Greek is literally "within you"

God does not delight in evil but rejoices with the truth. He always protects, always trusts, always hopes, always perseveres. God never fails! Corinthians 13:4-8[29]

We may worship or serve God but do we know who he is? What kind of character does he have or are we viewing God as an impersonal force full of all power and might but no heart?

God's heart is seen in scripture early on,

The LORD regretted that he had made human beings on the earth, and his heart was deeply troubled. Genesis 6:6

God was grieved because the people he had made were sinning greatly. God has feelings. We were made in his image not the other way, round so if we have deep feelings and emotions, how much more so does God have?

My fear reached its peak. As I was worshipping one morning, I had a very clear picture. I was running in fear away from an evil creature that was chasing me. In my picture, I stopped running and turned and faced the thing. It stopped dead in its tracks, froze on the spot, dropped its tail and ran off in the other direction. The shot then moved like a camera would in a film to focus on me facing the camera. A giant figure, reaching far into the sky stood behind me. Father God had my back. It was him the nasty creature had run from. This image to this day is still etched in my mind. I am not the one confronting my enemies, God is. It was from this moment fear began to lose its grip on me.

There is no fear in love. But perfect love drives out fear, because fear has to do with punishment. The one who fears is not made perfect in love. 1 John 4:18

As I set my heart on knowing God it was as though a barrier was taken away. A week after the picture I described above I heard this,

"Jenna you do things for me but won't you come **to**[30] me." And a few days after that, "Jenna your life is a testimony to my goodness." And in this moment I remember feeling like pure bliss was being poured over me, it felt like it covered my entire body. I remember I didn't know whether to laugh or cry.

---

[29] Love or "it"-referring to love is substituted by God or him accordingly [30] It felt like God emphasized this word when he said it

When Moses asked God to show him his Glory, God said he would cause all his goodness to pass by Moses. God's glory is his goodness.[31] They cannot be separated. God's goodness is who he is. As we come to God he begins to show us his goodness.

Remember earlier when I talked about the fear of the Lord? It says this in Proverbs,

The fear of the Lord is the beginning of wisdom, and knowledge of the Holy One is understanding. Proverbs 9:10

Since I had allowed myself to submit to the fear of the Lord I was beginning to receive wisdom. My question was then, what was the end of wisdom?

My goal is that they may be encouraged in heart and united in love, so that they may have the full riches of complete understanding, in order that they may know the mystery of God, namely, Christ, in whom are hidden all the treasures of wisdom and knowledge.[32] Colossians 2:2-3

Jesus Christ is the fulfillment of wisdom. And Jesus is God himself given in love for all of us. God so loved the world that he gave his Son. I felt Holy Spirit said to me,

"I'm not a God that takes but a God who GIVES!" My journey now was to grow in love and unity in the Son. I began to ask God for a baptism of love. When I use the word baptism, I mean I wanted to be; immersed, saturated, consumed, and fully one with love. God is not a paranoid, obsessive lover. He is not selfish. He is fully loved, a lover who is giving of himself unconditionally in all goodness.

Shortly after this, I went to a conference in another city. At the first meeting, I remember longing for God. I worshipped with great desire and near the end of the worship the speaker came on stage, I don't remember everything but I heard him say,

---

[31] See Exodus 33:18-19
[32] Underlined for emphasis

"You are so hungry for God the fire is coming on you now!" He was pointing at me and as I realised this I began to burn. My whole body felt a great heat all over it, especially my head and chest. Father picked me out of the crowd and poured his love out, I couldn't wait, I was desperate. This was the first of many times I have felt this burning. It is God's love coming to me and burning out all that is not him and it is him giving me himself. The following morning as I sat in the crowd waiting for the next meeting to start, I perceived with my spiritual eyes a ring of fire circling the roof of the building, I thought, that's weird, could just be my imagination. However, during the introductions, the speaker onstage said the intercessors (prayer people) while praying in the morning had seen a ring of fire circling the building. It wasn't my imagination!

John said this about Jesus,

John answered them all, "I baptize you with water. But one who is more powerful than I will come, the straps of whose sandals I am not worthy to untie. He will baptize you with the Holy Spirit and fire. His winnowing fork is in his hand to clear his threshing floor and to gather the wheat into his barn, but he will burn up the <u>chaff</u> [33] with unquenchable fire." Mathew 3:11-12

In this metaphor, wheat represents those who come to Jesus. We are his harvest. Chaff is the dry, scaly, protective casings of the seeds of cereal grain, or other similar plants. So when the fire of Jesus comes to us, it burns away our outer coverings. We have many protective mechanisms we have accumulated as we learn how to cope in life. We all need something, I get it, who wants to be exposed? But when Jesus comes to us, he wants to be our covering and protection. His love begins to burn away all that separates us from him, because ultimately even though these coverings protect us they also separate us. We remain isolated in our shell of protection, even from the ones who love us the most.

---

[33] Underlined for emphasis

Being vulnerable is difficult and vulnerability became difficult the day Adam and Eve covered themselves from their Father God. The refining and uncovering process had just begun in me. Its purpose; is for me to become one with Christ. We often think of holiness as something we do, but no it is a place, it is Christ Himself. He said be[34] holy, not do holy. Everything that was happening in my life was the process of the fire burning away my chaff. This is a crucial part of our relationship yet many of us don't allow this process, we give up or by our own choice put out our hand and say,

"That's enough God, no more." He will honour our decision. We have freedom in this relationship and this is the risk God takes. Do we want him or not? Just like the son who demanded his inheritance from his father and ran away from home, squandering all he had been given. The father watches and waits for his son's return.[35] He does not go after him but gives him freedom to leave. Yes God holds on to us no matter what, but the posture of the one who holds us is rooted in great love and respect for our own will. After all, we were created in his image. God thinks of us, he longs for us. He has a heart and is a great lover, a jealous lover.[36] He wants for him and us to have it all. We have an invitation to "roll in the deep places". Psalm 42 says,

Deep calls to deep in the roar of your waterfalls; all your waves and breakers have swept over me. Psalm 42:7

Jesus was scarred for us. The love he has for us pierced him. He still bears those scars. What are we looking for? What are we waiting for? Come and live a life of love supreme dear ones, in the fiery love of the greatest one of all; our Father/Mother God, Jesus Christ and Holy Spirit.

---

[34] See 1 Peter 1:15-16
[35] See Luke 15:11-32
[36] See Deuteronomy 4:24

CHAPTER 6

Dare to Question

s I searched out God's character, issues of mistrust towards God surfaced. There were some things blocking my ability to believe God really was good. Each of us may have questions, experiences or theological understanding that hinder us in fully surrendering to the truth of God's goodness. I had three big ones; Hell as a place of eternal torment, women's place in God's plan, and did God really want to heal and why weren't people healed?

Ultimately what I think/believe is subjective. Ultimately, we all "see through the glass darkly." Ultimately what I believe to be true will go through the fire.

For we know in part and we prophesy in part...For now we see only a reflection as in a mirror; then we shall see face to face. Now I know in part; then I shall know fully, even as I am fully known. And now these three remain: faith, hope and love. But the greatest of these is love. 1 Corinthians 13:9-10, 12-13

For no one can lay any foundation other than the one already laid, which is Jesus Christ. If anyone builds on this foundation using gold, silver, costly stones, wood, hay or straw, their work will be shown for what it is, because the Day will bring it to light. It will be revealed with fire, and the fire will test the quality of each person's work. 1 Corinthians 3:11-13

It is wisdom to hold our theology lightly, it is wisdom to understand that we cannot know all things or be absolute in what we "work out" to believe. (This book is my work and one day it will be tested by fire.) Someone else in a different Christian stream may hold a different view on something, maybe they are right? At the centre is Christ. The Moravians were a community of people who had included amongst themselves members from different denominations. They lived by this value,

"In essentials, unity; in nonessentials, liberty; and in all things, love".

In my mind the essentials centre around, Christ who is God, who became flesh, his death on the cross and the resurrection and what this accomplished. All else are nonessentials. You can have a different understanding of all kinds of other things. You are free to. One day we are all going to know what the truth is perfectly and in the meantime, we have permission to explore our understanding of God and what scripture means. The Nicene Creed is a beautiful statement to base our unity around.

I believe in one God, the Father Almighty, Maker of heaven and earth, and of all things visible and invisible.

And in one Lord Jesus Christ, the only-begotten Son of God, begotten of the Father before all worlds; God of God, Light of Light, very God of very God; begotten, not made, being of one substance with the Father, by whom all things were made.

Who, for us men for our salvation, came down from heaven, and was incarnate by the Holy Spirit of the virgin Mary, and was made man; and was crucified also for us under Pontius Pilate; He suffered and was buried; and the third day He rose again, according to the Scriptures; and ascended into heaven, and sits on the right hand of the Father; and He shall come again, with glory, to judge the quick and the dead; whose kingdom shall have no end.

And I believe in the Holy Ghost, the Lord and Giver of Life; who proceeds from the Father [and the Son]; who with the Father and the Son together is worshipped and glorified; who spoke by the prophets.

And I believe one holy catholic and apostolic Church. I acknowledge one baptism for the remission of sins; and I look for the resurrection of the dead, and the life of the world to come. Amen[37]

I am a lover of truth and I do my best to stand with truth even if it is painful for me or difficult to understand. I believe God honours our sincerity for truth even when we get it wrong.

---

[37] Nicene Creed 381 AD. The amended version from the 325 AD original.

It is the posture of a submitted heart that pleases Jesus. Let me share an example of this.

A couple of women in the church I was attending wore headscarves. Now since this was a Salvation Army church it wasn't promoted or taught in any way that women must do this. In fact, the Salvation Army had been pioneers in the equality of women in the church for a long time. Women in the Salvation Army can have higher ranking than men, essentially giving some women leadership over men. But in my search to uncover what was true for women, I really questioned it all. It does indeed say in scripture that women should cover their heads.

But every woman who prays or prophesies with her head uncovered dishonors her head—it is the same as having her head shaved. For if a woman does not cover her head, she might as well have her hair cut off; but if it is a disgrace for a woman to have her hair cut off or her head shaved, then she should cover her head. 1 Corinthians 11:5-6

Now I understand there are certain hermeneutical applications we need to apply; the historical and cultural context and who the letter was written by and to whom. We can certainly apply these here and we would be enlightened in our understanding and perhaps reach certain conclusions however for me at this time I leaned heavily on my teacher, the Holy Spirit to explain things to me. So on a fateful Sunday afternoon with a heavy but submitted heart, I covered my head and sat down to pray and ask God if that was what he really wanted. I told him I would do it, even if no other young women covered their heads, I would. My desire to please Father was greater than my reputation or even what I thought of it myself. Quite honestly I was insulted by the idea and everything in me revolted against having my "freedom" taken away. As I sat there in my little purple sanctuary, I heard the still, small voice.

"Jenna look at that verse again, notice the word 'if'."

I read the verses again. The light dawned on me, **"if"** it is a disgrace for a woman to have her hair cut off or her head shaved... **then** she should cover her head. It wasn't shameful for women to have shaved heads in our culture... WAHOO I was off the hook! Oh the lightness in my heart that came! I didn't have a need to persuade the other women who wore headscarves of my "revelation" but I found freedom for myself and my conscience was clear before God. We can at times only follow the path set before us. We are not responsible for somebody else's relationship with God and ultimately no person or spiritual leader is responsible for us, we alone hold this responsibility. What did I learn from this experience? Reading scripture means allowing the one who wrote it, the Holy Spirit, to interpret it for me. Not for me to only use my own thinking to interpret it.

All Scripture is God-breathed and is useful for teaching, rebuking, correcting and training in righteousness. 2 Timothy 3:16

Scripture is God-breathed but this breath is living. The living breath comes upon scripture and breathes life today. Otherwise, it is indeed like any other book, words on a page and able to be interpreted, understood or misunderstood in any way by the reader. This is why we have so many differing understandings between us related to scripture.

I would like to point out an important point here. Jesus himself referred to the bible[38] as scripture. He did not call it the Word of God. Why? Because He is the Word of God! As John writes,

In the beginning was the Word, and the Word was with God, and the Word was God. John 1:1

Jesus said,

You study the Scriptures diligently because you think that in them you have eternal life. These are the very Scriptures that testify about me, yet you refuse to come to me to have life. John 5:39- 40

---

[38] Which in his time included parts of what we now call the Old Testament, the New Testament wasn't even in existence yet.

Jesus stresses the importance of pursuing **him**. Scripture is useful. For me it is the most reliable and tactile source I have to learn of God outside my own subjective experiences and understanding, yet I must pair this source with my living relationship with a God who is real and speaks to me. There is wisdom in not adding to scripture what is not included there. Jesus used scripture in his encounter with the accuser. He kept saying, it is written![39] If Jesus did that, how much more do I need to then! Yet my faith and trust is not in a book but in Christ who is my reality. I want these to be in the proper order. Otherwise, I run the risk of placing scripture in a position it doesn't belong, this would be called; idolatry.

I believe God sees the sincerity of our hearts in our desire to follow him. I want to share another example of a wrestle I had in my understanding of a portion of scripture and I want to preface this by emphasising that there really is the freedom to each have our own experience, understanding or revelation of God and scripture. Only our righteous Judge, the Father can accurately discern and know what is in a person's heart and only he perfectly understands scripture.

I have been married at the time of writing to my wonderful husband for fifteen years. We have a delightful marriage and my husband is a precious gift given to me by our Father. At the time of our engagement, a dear family member wrote me an email citing his concerns about my upcoming marriage. You see my husband had been previously married and for this dear person, this meant my husband was not free to marry according to his understanding of scripture. I have a very sensitive heart and I was troubled by this email. I didn't respond to the email immediately nor did I feel angry, but what I wanted was complete peace in my understanding of this issue. I wanted to hear from the Holy Spirit. I had a night shift at work so I had the entire day to sit in God's presence and hear from him.

[39] See Mathew 4:1-11

I remember feeling extremely burdened like a heavy, dark thing was draped over me. It was quite awful to sit there and read through scripture and try to make sense of it all. If I had come to the conclusion that it really was wrong in God's eyes then I wouldn't marry my love.

Due to the sensitive nature of this and to protect the people involved, I will not tell all the details but I will highlight the point where the moment of clarity came for me as I studied and meditated on the scriptures. It came from this verse where Jesus is speaking,

You have heard that it was said, 'You shall not commit adultery. But I tell you that anyone who looks at a woman lustfully has already committed adultery with her in his heart. Mathew 5:27-28

In essence, if we look at someone with lust, we have committed adultery. A few verses later Jesus condemns the people for divorcing so easily and he says that adultery is the only reasonable exemption from this.[40] In Jesus' eyes adultery is the only reason to divorce, yet a few verses earlier he is saying that if we have lust in our heart then we have committed adultery. Therefore, following this logic we are all in the line of fire to be divorced from our significant other. Who hasn't had lust in their hearts? What person can say they have never eyed somebody else, even if it passes quickly through the mind with no agreement or action associated with the thought. And so in that moment, it was not about me critiquing the situation and determining if "by law" I could marry (which in the circumstances I actually could) but rather Holy Spirit pointed out my own position as an adulterer! Think of that. I was in need of grace and grace I can receive and therefore grace I give to all just as I have been given it.

The weight of the question lifted from me and I sensed glorious freedom as I understood how high God's ways really are and how much we are all in need of mercy and the chance for restoration.

---

40 See Mathew 5:31-32

We get stuck in questions of law yet the Holy Spirit is always pointing us to the higher way of love that transcends and fulfills the law.

Let us go back to the "dare to question" theme, it is a fearful thing to question what we have been taught, especially if the majority of people we associate with or the church or spiritual community we belong to follow the same belief structures, ideas and theology. It is even more difficult if what we hear from behind the pulpit is proclaimed to be the absolute truth and there is an unspoken feeling that to question something is to be in defiance against authority. I would like to suggest that it is always right to question and think for ourselves, otherwise we are surrendering to control.

Guidance is one thing, control belongs in the category of being cultish and abusive. If my spiritual community is healthy, it will encourage questions and differences of opinion and these do not disrupt the unity of the group but rather enhance growth and maturity.

At my young age of questioning it was difficult to leave the "security of the group," even if it was only in theological positions. My ground felt shaky, what was I standing on? Looking back this time brought tremendous growth to my spiritual life and I see in hindsight that it was a springboard to deeper places in God. A whole new world of possibilities opened and the expansiveness of our Creator became more real than ever. I had to face the unknown; the fear of the unknown and entrust myself to the God of love. What I was actually losing was faith in my own faith. What I was gaining was grace. Grace to let go and not know or understand everything. Grace to let God be God.

Be completely humble and gentle; be patient, bearing with one another in love. Make every effort to keep the unity of the Spirit through the bond of peace. There is one body and one Spirit, just as you were called to one hope when you were called; one Lord, one faith, one baptism; one God and Father of all, who is over all and through all and in all. But to each one of us grace has been given as Christ apportioned it. Ephesians 4:1-7

The point I sense the Holy Spirit wants to highlight is in everything it's about becoming one with him. We cannot become one with someone we don't trust and if we have hurt, questions or unbelief God wants to come to those places and say something. Even if we don't receive a specific answer (which is what I would prefer) or find comfort or healing in our area of need then at least we find God there. We find a loving parent who does want to answer our questions if she deems it good for us, or at the very least comfort us in the area of doubt enough so that we are able to rest in the "mystery". As turbulent as this time was for me my foundations were being deconstructed and built back together. As Jesus said, unless our house is built on the rock- himself, how will we last the storms of life?[41] And so I dared to question and I dared to lose everything to gain what I really wanted; God himself, not theology, not ritual or religious activity. In the process deep seated ways and thought processes were being unearthed, the thoughts of my heart, thoughts hidden to me were being dug up. Some would call these strongholds. Some of what I was finding was not so pleasant. However, deliverance out of some of these strongholds was coming my way.

---

[41] Luke 6:46-49 Doing what Jesus tells us means coming into a trust relationship with Him.

CHAPTER 7

Choosing life

I read a lot of books at this time, these paragraphs from a book of Rick Joyner struck at my core and like a laser beam narrowed in on a shocking issue I had I wasn't aware of,

"The martyr syndrome is one of the ultimate and most deadly delusions when combined with the religious spirit. To be a true martyr for the faith, to literally lose our life for the sake of Christ, is one of the greatest honours that we can receive in this life. When this is perverted it is a most tragic form of deception. When a religious spirit is combined with the martyr syndrome it is almost impossible for that person to be delivered from the deception that he is suffering for the gospel. At this point any rejection or correction is perceived as the price he must pay to 'stand for the truth.' This will drive him even further from the truth and any possibility of correction.

The martyr syndrome can also be a manifestation of the spirit of suicide. It is sometimes easier to 'die for the Lord' than it is to live for him. Those who have a perverted understanding of the cross glory more in death than they do in life. The point of the cross is the resurrection not the grave."[42]

I realised I gloried more in death than life. Secretly a part of me wanted to die and not have to struggle in life anymore and now since Jesus had me, death was not final, I would carry on living in heaven. Even all the struggle I felt I went through was because "this is what it was to suffer for Christ".

I was comforted in my feelings of rejection for being a Christian,

[42] Epic battles of the Last Days by Rick Joyner, published by Morning Star Ministries 1995

Oh look at me, the most righteous of sufferers. I was now confronted with my reality, death was closer to me than life. I needed to make a choice.

Now what I am commanding you today is not too difficult for you or beyond your reach. It is not up in heaven, so that you have to ask, "Who will ascend into heaven to get it and proclaim it to us so we may obey it?" Nor is it beyond the sea, so that you have to ask, "Who will cross the sea to get it and proclaim it to us so we may obey it?" No, the word is very near you; it is in your mouth and in your heart so you may obey it. See, I set before you today life and prosperity, death and destruction. For I command you today to love the LORD your God, to walk in obedience to him, and to keep his commands, decrees and laws; then you will live and increase, and the LORD your God will bless you in the land you are entering to possess. Deuteronomy 30:11-16

This day I call the heavens and the earth as witnesses against you that I have set before you life and death, blessings and curses. <u>Now choose life</u>[43], so that you and your children may live and that you may love the LORD your God, listen to his voice, and hold fast to him. For the LORD is your life, and he will give you many years in the land he swore to give to your fathers, Abraham, Isaac and Jacob. Deuteronomy 30:19-20

In my journal in May of 2002, I wrote these words,

This day God my Father, I make a choice to choose life. I choose life today. I choose to walk in your ways. I choose to embrace life. To believe in life. To hope in life. To love in life. You are the Almighty and by your might, your truth, your Spirit and your blood. In fact just by your very word, you have broken the power of death over my life. Thank-you for setting me free. Help me Holy Spirit to walk by your life. To convict my words and attitudes, my thoughts and my ways that you would grant me to choose life. Let your words be in my heart and mouth. That I would speak blessing over myself and others. Thank-you that you never leave me, that you speak

---

43 Underlined for emphasis

to me and that you counsel me in the way I should go. I love you my darling Spirit, you are mine and I am yours. Thank-you for your protection.

These processes I have been describing were occurring simultaneously. It was the weekend after choosing life that I went to the conference and saw the fire of God circling the building. If God pulls things down in us, he then re-builds and restores us and since he is outside our four dimensional time he is able to build in ways we have not imagined. Our spirit is made in his image. Think how layered and multi-dimensional our spirit really is then. It's no wonder our emotions, thoughts and our bodies, in fact, our entire being can barely keep up when God is doing major reconstruction work in us.

The choices we make allow God to work in us. He guides us and instructs us but he does not make our choices for us. As I chose life I opened myself to all the possibilities this choice contained while at the same time shutting the door on some unfavorable influences- namely: death, rejection and self-pity. I still remember the moment I received freedom from these. It was some four months later, I was visiting a church and the speaker said he felt the river of God was flowing and if we wanted to get in the river we should come up the front. Of course, we couldn't see a physical river but I certainly felt it like wind around me and as a feeling of peace. As I stood there sucking it up I longed for the tremendous peace I felt to be a permanent feeling in my life. The speaker came over to me and began to pray, he asked that rejection, death and self-pity would be removed from me. As he said this it was as though a lightbulb went off in my head, I thought, no I don't want it (specifically I meant self-pity) anymore. The moment I had that thought I felt a dark thing lifting off my head. I literally felt the movement as it departed and the lightness that was left. I had no idea I was being afflicted with self-pity and the heaviness, introspection and depression it was causing me. I had been aware of the rejection and death but the self-pity, that had been hidden.

Note, it wasn't until I agreed with the person praying that I didn't want self-pity that it left me. We are often in agreement with darkness even if it is unknowingly. Self-pity is the opposite of love, love is not self-seeking. Self-pity was blocking me from experiencing love's fullness and from enjoying my life. I was constantly wishing for what I didn't have, instead of seeing what I DID have. This kind of thought life destroys joy, it destroys hope and it shuns love. For me especially it sucked my energy as my thoughts dwelt on the things I didn't have or what bad things might happen to me. Now we can all have these thoughts from time to time but mine had become consistent and this I believe opened the way for a demonic spirit to oppress me. Although not on the inside of me, since the Holy Spirit dwelt in my spirit, the oppression was attached to wounded parts of my soul.

There is a lot of confusion in the body of Christ regarding these things and I wholeheartedly believe when we surrender to Jesus we enter into new life. The old has gone the new has come.[44] Yet we don't always feel the new yet or are walking in it. This does not negate our newness rather it is in the same line of being as the nature of God who describes himself,

"I am the Alpha and the Omega," says the Lord God, "who is, and who was, and who is to come, the Almighty." Revelation 1:8

Our logic thinks in terms of a linear line namely in the dimension of time. God is beyond time. We enter into this same state; of being beyond time when we come into union with Christ. Therefore I can say I am already made new and I am being made new. I am already holy and I am being made holy. Remember that holiness is a place, the person of God. To be made holy is to be set apart to and with him. There is no conflict in these concepts as we learn the ways of God.

"For my thoughts are not your thoughts, neither are your ways my ways,"

declares the LORD. "As the heavens are higher than the earth, so are my ways higher than your ways and my thoughts than your thoughts. Isaiah 55:8-9

[44] See 2 Corinthians 5:17

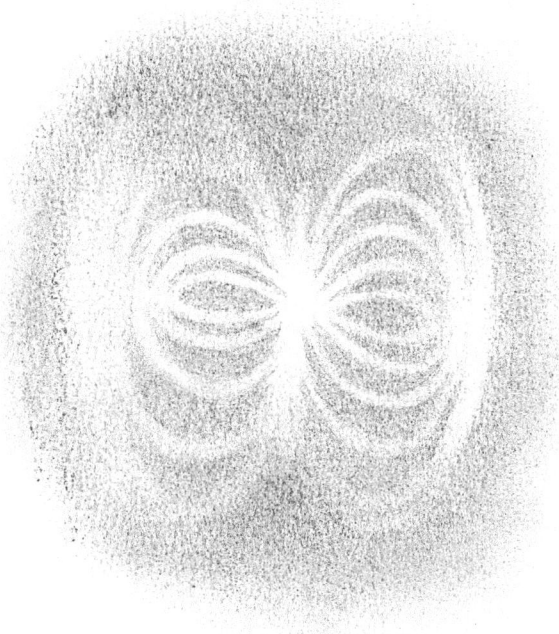

In this process of choosing life, I felt God asking me to remember where I had come from. In essence that I had pre-existed somehow before I was born on earth. I am not saying I am eternal. There is only one who is uncreated or unbegotten-God. But I felt as though since I came from God I somehow entered into existence before taking up residence in my physical body. Maybe God created my spirit first and then placed it in the physical body prepared for me. Who knows?

However, God is my home and I came from her. This journey in the material world is important and yet not the whole picture. My days were ordained for me before I was born.

Your eyes saw my unformed body; all the days ordained[45] for me were written in your book before one of them came to be. Psalm 139:16

So here we see God had plans for us from the beginning. It's incredible to think of this. A life of meaning and purpose. I can be and do what was specially designed and crafted for me, a life of fulfillment on every level. By choosing life I opened myself to the plan God had for me and allowed him to direct my path more specifically. Not everything that happens to us is God's plan, the free- will of others and the imperfection of this world warps the original intentions. The more I am able to join with Father, the more his perfect plan can overcome and restore the distortions. My own plans needed to be removed first and then I was ready to hear what Father had in store for me. This is a choice. His love for us does not diminish when we choose our own way. Yet we limit ourselves due to a lack of really understanding ourselves. There is one who knows us perfectly, how much wisdom is there in following the advice and plan of one such as this? And we do have someone who knows us, it was she who created us, our wonderful God-parent!

One Saturday morning as I was hanging out in the living room I felt an urge to go very specifically to my room and pray. I had already spent time with God that morning and I wondered why the urge, it was unusual. As I shut the door of my little purple sanctuary, the presence of God filled the room. I even knelt by my bed, something I never normally did and I saw in my mind a vision of myself writing. I was writing what God was doing in a generation, specifically the youth generation. Earlier I had begun to sense my call was not to the third-world nations as I had previously thought but to the first-world nations. It was all I saw in that moment and I interpreted it as me writing about miracles and God's exploits, since I craved to be in this kind of action. Often when God shows us something we do not understand it fully, such as was my case here.

The other thing about this experience was I felt like God was literally in the room. I didn't often sense him like that.

---

45 The dictionary has one of the definitions for ordained as 'ordered by fate or God'.

I had no idea what to do with my vision. God knew what he was up to though. A few days later my alarm woke me up for work. Except it wasn't playing a music CD the way it normally would but the radio came on. (I still don't know how this happened, it must have been you know who LOL) The first thing I heard upon waking was an advertisement for a Journalism school. I heard the Holy Spirit say to me,

"That's where you are going." The sudden of God happened. I applied to the school, and I got accepted. I did not have money and nor was I prepared to get a student loan for it but God had that figured out also as I got a job alongside my flatmate at a plastics factory over the summer and Christmas holidays which ended up paying so much overtime/holiday pay that I was able to save the whole sum of my student fees. My capacity to organise myself at this time was atrocious as I was still recovering from my burn out. I found a place to live by placing one singular advertisement in a church newsletter of one church in the city I was to move to one week before I was supposed to start school. I got a phone call from a young lady saying she had a room available. The rent and costs were perfect for me. I learnt that Father really does take care of us. I was not responsible, I hardly did anything to try to find that place to live but I had that one idea of placing the advertisement, (It would have been God's idea) it worked out. And very like God 'at the eleventh hour' as we say.

God would not appreciate it so much if I would behave in the same way these days, since I have been growing up in him but like in the natural a young child needs more support than an older one. The Father is like that with us. He treats us according to where we are in the growth process. He knows where we are and what our capacities are. He came and took care of his young girl, even when she did fall asleep in the sun the day she was supposed to scout out accommodation options in the new city of the Journalism school.

A major hindrance in choosing life can hang on the mistrust we have towards God. If God has such a great plan for my life then why did ...(you can fill this space here with any tragic, difficult or horrendous thing) happen to me/in my life. And especially incidences occurring during our childhood when we had little control or choice. The question of why is huge and I will in no way attempt to answer or speculate. I want to offer however a disclaimer. Since we are humans with free choice many choices we make are not good. Our parents may make wrong choices affecting us. We do live in an imperfect place where there is sickness and death, yet does not the same things happen to all indiscriminately, as the proverbial saying goes, the rain falls on the good and the bad. I had my own questions, why did I suffer illness frequently as a child and have open heart surgery at the age of seven? Why did my father suffer under the alcoholic abuse of his father? In recent years as I have become more whole, I have at times heard the Holy Spirit ask forgiveness from me for certain things that have happened. I have felt the compassion of God towards me and her pain at what I have suffered. Ultimately the heart of God is sad for us and he is with us when we go through pain and trauma, it is not his heart. God would want to shelter us all from suffering and yet our freedom of choice is more important to God.

And we know that in all things God works for the good of those who love him, who have been called according to his purpose. Romans 8:28

In my sufferings, I have felt the nearness of God. His work of restoration in me is to bring me healing and peace no matter what I have been through and will go through. The promise is that no matter what, good has to come to come out of ALL things including the terrible things. This does not suggest God planned the bad things...NO! But his justice means in harm, the good must come. This is the redemptive nature of God and this redemption is being worked out in us no matter what we have gone through and experienced willingly or unwillingly. Even our own bad choices God uses for our good. Will I trust God? One might call this surrender. I surrender to Father all my emotions. I choose to not hold bitterness against God but believe God is actually on my side. I cannot say it better than the scripture verses directly following the one quoted above,

For those God foreknew he also predestined to be conformed to the image of his Son, that he might be the firstborn among many brothers and sisters. And those he predestined, he also called; those he called, he also justified; those he justified, he also glorified. What, then, shall we say in response to these things? If God is for us, who can be against us? He who did not spare his own Son, but gave him up for us all—how will he not also, along with him, graciously give us all things? Who will bring any charge against those whom God has chosen? It is God who justifies.

Who then is the one who condemns? No one. Christ Jesus who died—more than that, who was raised to life—is at the right hand of God and is also interceding for us Who shall separate us from the love of Christ? Shall trouble or hardship or persecution or famine or nakedness or danger or sword? As it is written: "For your sake we face death all day long; we are considered as sheep to be slaughtered." No, in all these things we are more than conquerors through him who loved us. For I am convinced that neither death nor life, neither angels nor demons, neither the present nor the future, nor any powers, neither height nor depth, nor anything else in all creation, will be able to separate us from the love of God that is in Christ Jesus our Lord.

Romans 8:29-39

God believed in me enough to place me in this world. He risked himself and his reputation to plant me here in an imperfect world hoping that I would somehow still reach out for him and believe that he really is a good and loving God. A God who not only loves me but gives me all things. He did not leave me alone here to battle it out and survive all the desperation but gave me himself and gave me the commission to bear his image and take authority over the earth.[46]

This has not been easy for me. The child in me had a lot of fear, and the

---

[46] See God's command to Adam and Eve in Genesis 1:26-28

teenager in me had a lot of anger and hate. Emotional wounds cripple us and make it difficult to rise up and be the people we were created to be. This is exactly the journey God has us on. Becoming the new creation means allowing God to nurture us into wholeness. My place in him-holiness is a state of becoming without blemish or defect. My wounds become gold. We are refined and in the places in ourselves we are most disturbed by, these are the places where the most beauty shines from, since it is from these places God has deposited himself.

But God chose the foolish things of the world to shame the wise; God chose the weak things of the world to shame the strong. God chose the lowly things of this world and the despised things— and the things that are not—to nullify the things that are, so that no one may boast before him. 1 Corinthians 27-29

Praise be to the God and Father of our Lord Jesus Christ! In his great mercy he has given us new birth into a living hope through the resurrection of Jesus Christ from the dead, and into an inheritance that can never perish, spoil or fade. This inheritance is kept in heaven for you, who through faith are shielded by God's power until the coming of the salvation that is ready to be revealed in the last time. In all this you greatly rejoice, though now for a little while you may have had to suffer grief in all kinds of trials. These have come so that the proven genuineness of your faith—of greater worth than gold, which perishes even though refined by fire—may result in praise, glory and honor when Jesus Christ is revealed. 1 Peter 1:3-7

Life is a precious gift given to us. You are alive! Think of it, this is not meant to sound heavy but we are responsible for growing up in this life and enjoying and using what we have been given. Jesus teaches us in parables[47] about this saying how we will give an account. Don't forget our loving Father measures/judges us rightly and understands where we are in our growth process.

He will and does help us. We are not alone in this life and it is the orphan

---

[47] See Mathew 25:15-30, Luke 12:35-48, etc. Jesus emphasised the responsibility we have and affirmed the authority given to us by the Father in the beginning.

in us who becomes burdened with life instead of finding joy in life as we are supposed to. Remember the experience I had where the Holy Spirit kept whispering to me,

"Never will I leave you, never will I forsake you." She does not expect us to cope on our own. God expects us to lean into her and receive all we need. God is our Life. Jesus is our life, we are in glorious union with him and that is why we can rise up and live. The Spirit is breathing over some of you,

"LIVE!" She is shouting and roaring, "LIVE!" We see this picture here,

On the day you were born your cord was not cut, nor were you washed with water to make you clean, nor were you rubbed with salt or wrapped in cloths. No one looked on you with pity or had compassion enough to do any of these things for you. Rather, you were thrown out into the open field, for on the day you were born you were despised. " 'Then I passed by and saw you kicking about in your blood, and as you lay there in your blood I said to you, "Live!" I made you grow like a plant of the field. You grew and developed and entered puberty. Your breasts had formed and your hair had grown, yet you were stark naked. " 'Later I passed by, and when I looked at you and saw that you were old enough for love, I spread the corner of my garment over you and covered your naked body. I gave you my solemn oath and entered into a covenant with you, declares the Sovereign LORD, and you became mine. " 'I bathed you with water and washed the blood from you and put ointments on you. I clothed you with an embroidered dress and put sandals of fine leather on you. I dressed you in fine linen and covered you with costly garments. I adorned you with jewelry: I put bracelets on your arms and a necklace around your neck, and I put a ring on your nose, earrings on your ears and a beautiful crown on your head. Ezekiel 16:4- 12

Even if our beginning in life is under the most tragic or horrific of circumstances there was another who had ultimate authority over us, our true parent-God. God has the final say and he says we are alive!

CHAPTER 8

Healing the great divide

What we believe determines our thoughts, feelings and actions. For example, if I believed the world would end in five years, this would dramatically change the way I live my life now. I wouldn't be writing this book. There would be no need to invest in the future generations. My philosophy and understanding of this world shapes how I live in it and determines my values and priorities. God was now digging at some core beliefs in me, in order to exchange them for his beliefs. In my christian circles, there seemed to be a prevailing thought whether conscious or unconscious, "Spirit is good, matter or the body is bad."

Studying journalism placed me right in the center of human activity: school, fellow students (the majority of whom were not following Jesus), study disciplines, local council meetings (I joined the youth city council), police reports, political issues, etc... the list could go on. After all my fervour in following spiritual things, God had placed me right in the middle of human things, wait, is this statement true? Why would human things not be spiritual things? And it is here that I am confronted with the question. Why this dualism, this great divide between spirit and matter? Did God really think our daily human life is not important, was he absent from aspects of my life? This kind of dualistic thinking first affected me in my initial pursuit of God. I would lock myself up in my room for my "God time" and then come out and try to live the rest of my day without a sense of burden. I had found great contentment in my secret place with God and everything else was a struggle, I felt burdened by responsibility. During my student days at Journalism school, I obviously wasn't completely well from the burn-out, this manifested in my body, I would get dizzy and need to lie down. Especially on my days off, it was as though all the stress was waiting for me and I couldn't relax. Looking back I realise I also had a lot of tension in my neck and shoulders, this might have contributed but it was weird how I was most exhausted on the days I had off. It was as though I felt a whip at my back, do more Jenna, get more done, be efficient. The bondage of "doing" lingered.

I felt the tension of being Mary or Martha.[48] I only wanted to sit at Jesus's feet. But I needed to do practical things. Why could I not just be Mary? This was the longing of my heart, I wanted God. I wanted spiritual things, the "better" things. I often complained to God,

"I want to always be with you." I just couldn't understand his answer,

"But I am with you." I didn't feel God was with me all the time. All I could feel was my responsibilities, the burden of people, the groan of injustice and the crappy stuff of humanity confronting me at every turn. This scripture seemed entirely untrue,

And they were calling to one another: "Holy, holy, holy is the Lord Almighty; the whole earth is full of his glory."[49]Isaiah 6:3

How could the earth be full of God's glory? What I saw was pain, suffering, destruction and so on. Yet either scripture was wrong or I was and clearly we know which one was wrong. The seraphim are not lying when they say the whole earth is full of God's glory. I needed my vision to be healed to see what was true. I had glasses tinted by my own misconceptions. In the beginning, God said what he made was good, but I obviously was not in agreement. To me things were not good, they were messed up. Our beautiful God has a perspective that is timeless, his thoughts do not change,

---

[48] See Luke 10:38-42
[49] Underlined for emphasis

God is not human, that he should lie, not a human being, that he should

change his mind. Does he speak and then not act? Does he promise and not fulfill?
Numbers 23:19

The seraphim were saying this in the time before Christ when the law and sin still reigned. Clearly, then it wasn't a perception based on the state of humankind but rather the eternal perspective of God and his own glory and goodness. When God spoke and said, "Let there be light", the light of God filled the known universe, or the dimension where matter resides (the reality we see and understand). Jesus said he is the light of the world, all things were made by him[50]. Christ says he shares the same glory as the Father,

And now, Father, glorify me in your presence with the glory I had with you
before the world began. John 17:5

It was this light and glory that filled the known universe. What is the glory of God exactly? The Hebrew word for glory is kabowd, the concordance definition for this word is, *properly, weight, but only figuratively in a good sense, splendor or copiousness:—glorious(-ly), glory, honour(-able).*

How does God define his glory?

Then Moses said, "Now show me your glory[51]." And the LORD said, "I will cause all my goodness[52] to pass in front of you, and I will proclaim my name, the LORD, in your presence. I will have mercy on whom I will have mercy, and I will have compassion on whom I will have compassion. Exodus 33:18-19

Moses asked to see God's glory and God responded by saying he would cause all his goodness to pass before Moses. God equates his glory with his goodness. Those seraphim were in essence saying the whole earth was full of his goodness and this was my problem. Father was trying to help me have his perspective, the truth. The earth is full of his glory and goodness. Would I have the heart to see? Paul prays that the eyes of our hearts would be enlightened,

---

50 See John 1:1-4
51 Underlined for emphasis
52 Underlined for emphasis

I pray that the eyes of your heart may be enlightened in order that you may know the hope to which he has called you, the riches of his glorious inheritance in his holy people...Ephesians 1:18

Part of this hope to which he has called us is in accurately perceiving the truth of God's goodness. Is the light of God expanding and filling the universe or do I have an understanding that says darkness is increasing and the world is getting worse? How could it be getting worse if in the times of Isaiah, the seraphim proclaimed the glory of God under the shadow of death and yet we are living in the victory of the resurrected Christ? Would it not be logical to say there is more glory now than when it was proclaimed in Isaiah's time? Yes I know, Jesus said the darkness would increase but the light will also increase. He spoke these things in parables to his disciples.[53] Jesus understood the prophecy of the prophet Daniel,

While you were watching, a rock was cut out, but not by human hands. It struck the statue on its feet of iron and clay and smashed them. Then the iron, the clay, the bronze, the silver and the gold were all broken to pieces and became like chaff on a threshing floor in the summer. The wind swept them away without leaving a trace. But the rock that struck the statue became a huge mountain and filled the whole earth. Daniel 2:34-35 Daniel explains his vision,

"In the time of those kings, the God of heaven will set up a kingdom that will never be destroyed, nor will it be left to another people. It will crush all those kingdoms and bring them to an end, but it will itself endure forever. This is the meaning of the vision of the rock cut out of a mountain, but not by human hands—a rock that broke the iron, the bronze, the clay, the silver and the gold to pieces. Daniel 2:44-45

The rock is Christ![54] He was not made by human hands, he has set up a new kingdom rule.

[53] See Jesus's parables concerning the kingdom of God. Especially Mathew 13:24-30 and the growing kingdom of God/light Mathew 13:31-32

[54] See, the stone I have set in front of Joshua! There are seven eyes on that one stone, and I will engrave an inscription on it,' says the LORD Almighty, 'and I will remove the sin of this land in a single day. Zechariah 3:9 This verse is speaking of Christ. Again, Christ is called the stone here, As it is written: "See, I lay in Zion a stone that causes people to stumble and a rock that makes them fall, and the one who believes in him will never be put to shame. Romans 9:33

His kingdom is the everlasting kingdom, the one that cannot be destroyed and becomes a huge mountain and fills the earth. If his kingdom fills the whole earth then light fills the whole earth because he IS the light of the world. Darkness is operating but the light of God fills the earth, has filled the earth and is filling the earth. Here it is again, the eternal perspective of standing outside time and seeing the past, present and future as one. This is how Holy Spirit wanted me to see. He wanted me to see the light and glory and goodness of God in and through everything. Standing in this light, the whole world changes. If we see something that is not in the light and full of goodness then we have the mandate to help the light shine. We are Jesus Christ's ambassadors bringing and being this message of light[55].

Where does the dualistic thinking come from that says matter is bad, spirit is good? I found the best explanation from the website of the Jewish Virtual Library, a project by AICE,

"In the history of Western thought, philosophical dualism goes back to *Platonism and *neoplatonism which developed and spread the idea of an opposition between spirit and matter, spirit being the higher, purer, and eternal principle, whereas matter was the lower and imperfect form of being, subject to change and corruption. Applied to the understanding of the nature of man, this meant that man was composed of a lower, material part (the body), and a higher, spiritual part (the soul). This dualism could, and not infrequently did, lead to a contempt for the body and for "this world" in general, and encouraged a moral outlook which held *asceticism (or, in its more extreme forms, total renunciation of the world) to be the way by which the soul could liberate itself from the hold of the body and, purifying itself of the bodily passions, render itself worthy again of returning to its celestial and spiritual home.

[55] See 2 Corinthians 5:20

This view exerted considerable influence on Jewish thinking in the Hellenistic period (see *Philo) and in the philosophy and *Musar literature of the middle ages, though its more radical forms were partly inhibited by the rabbinic tradition which considered the physical universe and its enjoyment as essentially good, provided they were hallowed in the service of God."[56]

Jewish Rabbinic tradition considered the physical world as good and as something to be enjoyed under God's favour. This aligns with the declaration of God in Genesis when he declared his creation to be good. It was the Greek philosopher Plato born some 428/427 years before Christ who introduced the idea that the body was "lower" than the soul. Yet Jesus Christ affirmed the beauty of all aspects of humanity, look at what he taught,

Jesus called the crowd to him and said, "Listen and understand. What goes into someone's mouth does not defile them, but what comes out of their mouth, that is what defiles them." Then the disciples came to him and asked, "Do you know that the Pharisees were offended when they heard this?" He replied, "Every plant that my heavenly Father has not planted will be pulled up by the roots. Leave them; they are blind guides. If the blind lead the blind, both will fall into a pit." Peter said, "Explain the parable to us."

"Are you still so dull?" Jesus asked them. "Don't you see that whatever enters the mouth goes into the stomach and then <u>out of the body?</u>[57] But the things <u>that come out of a person's mouth come from the heart, and these defile them.</u>[58] For out of the heart come evil thoughts—murder, adultery, sexual immorality, theft, false testimony, slander. These are what defile a person; but eating with unwashed hands does not defile them." Mathew 15:10-20

---

[56] https://www.jewishvirtuallibrary.org/dualism
[57] Underlined for emphasis
[58] Underlined for emphasis

Jesus said it is not what comes out of the body that defiles them, but what comes out of the heart. Jesus did not put down bodily things, in fact he healed bodies! He turned water into wine[59], a miracle that some might deem wasn't important yet Jesus celebrated in the wedding and gave the people joyful drink. He feasted with people and was criticised by the pharisees for being a glutton and drunkard.[60]

It appears to my mind the pharisees were more "greek" in their thinking in the way they despised bodily things, they seem to be more "ascetic" than jewish in the way they spoke about the body and life in general. Jesus seems to act the opposite to restore healthy thinking and understanding of the world and the way humanity lives in it. The way HE created it to be. The greatest example Jesus gave was in the fact, he, the Creator of all, became human. I cannot say it better than scripture,

In your relationships with one another, have the same mindset as Christ Jesus: Who, being in very nature God, did not consider equality with God something to be used to his own advantage; rather, he made himself nothing by taking the very nature of a servant, being made in human likeness. And being found in appearance as a man, he humbled himself by becoming obedient to death— even death on a cross! Philippians 2:5-8

You see it's not that we need to ascend to heaven, for God came down to us! In Christ heaven and earth, the spiritual and the material are made one and if we are in Christ then we have this unity within us. We are spiritual and material, there is no separation. Jesus said this,

He then added, "Very truly I tell you, you will see 'heaven open, and the angels of God ascending and descending on' the Son of Man." John 1:51

Jesus was speaking about himself and was referring to Jacob's ladder in Genesis,

[59] See John 2:1-11
[60] See Mathew 11:19

Jacob left Beersheba and set out for Harran. When he reached a certain place, he stopped for the night because the sun had set. Taking one of the stones there, he put it under his head and lay down to sleep. He had a dream in which he saw a stairway resting on the earth, with its top reaching to heaven, and the angels of God were ascending and descending on it. Genesis 28:10-12

Jesus is the ladder that connects heaven and earth. He modeled what it looks like to walk with our feet on the earth and be in a relationship with our Father in heaven. Just as eternity is a concept difficult for us, so is the concept of heaven and earth being one. Ponder these statements by Jesus for a moment,

"My prayer is not for them alone. I pray also for those who will believe in me through their message, that all of them may be one, Father, just as <u>you are in me</u> and <u>I am in you.</u>[61] May <u>they also be in us</u>[62] so that the world may believe that you have sent me. I have given them the glory that you gave me, that they may be one as we are one—<u>I in them and you in me</u>[63]—so that they may be brought to complete unity. Then the world will know that you sent me and have loved them even as you have loved me." John 17:20-23

OK, so if we look at the underlined parts above we see that; The Father is IN Jesus and Jesus is IN the Father. We are IN the Father and Jesus; who is one, and all of Jesus followers are one as the Father and Jesus are one and Jesus is IN us. And deeper in, the Father is IN Jesus who is IN us. This feels like a circle or spiral where there is no beginning or end to where one starts and one ends.

Who is in who and who is where? Welcome to the outstanding mystery of God and his relationship with himself and us.

Union or oneness is who God is, whether it be about the relationship between people and himself or whether it be the relationship between heaven and earth. Everything about God creates unity. This is the antithesis of the material/spirit duality.

---

[61] Underlined for emphasis
[62] Underlined for emphasis
[63] Underlined for emphasis

Holy Spirit was with me at my school, Holy Spirit was blessing and moving over all my activities related to it. I just didn't get it. I had had hints of God's presence being everywhere prior to my attending school. One incident still stands out clearly in my mind.

In my home city, I often went to a gig venue where all kinds of bands played. It was a venue underage people could attend since it was an alcohol-free zone. I remember during one band's song set I could feel the presence of God. I raised my hands in worship exhilarated by the truth that God was happily present there. It wasn't church. It wasn't a church event, it wasn't run by Christians. Yet I was encountering my God. Why? Because I am the church, we are the church.

When the Holy Spirit comes and takes up home in us, we become a walking heaven. We carry God with us everywhere. Even before Jesus came, God was near, remember this verse?

No, the word is very near you; it is in your mouth and in your heart so you may obey it. Deuteronomy 30:14

How much more so when Holy Spirt lives inside us. We don't have to move one step or say one prayer to get any closer to God. We are as close as we will ever be to this side of eternity.[64] The curtain in the Jewish temple was torn the moment Christ died[65]. The Holy of Holies, the place where the manifest presence of God dwelt was laid bare. He was coming out of hiding![66] The rocks split, the earth shook, and a major shift was taking place. Not only did God come out of hiding but 40 days after the resurrection of Jesus Christ, Holy Spirit, God herself came and filled the house and the 120 followers of Jesus, who were waiting as Jesus told them to.[67]

Why is it then we struggle so much to sense/feel God's nearness? It is because of our minds and our souls. Our minds are a battlefield. Paul was clear on this when he writes,

Once you were alienated from God and were enemies in your minds[68] because of your evil behavior. Colossians 1:21

The mind governed by the flesh is death, but the mind governed by the Spirit is life and peace. Romans 8:6

We demolish arguments and every pretension that sets itself up against the knowledge of God, and we take captive every thought to make it obedient to Christ. 2 Corinthians 10:5

Our minds, thoughts, will and feelings need to come in alignment with the Spirit. That's why Jesus said,

To the Jews who had believed him, Jesus said, "If you hold to my teaching, you are really my disciples. Then you will know the truth, and the truth will set you free[69]." John 8:31-32

---

[64] In "this side" of eternity, by this I mean the body we have now before we get a new body after physical death or the end of this age.
[65] See Mathew 27:51
[66] This process had began the moment Jesus was conceived in the womb of Mary.
[67] See Acts 2:1-3
[68] Underlined for emphasis
[69] Underlined for emphasis

When we KNOW[70] the truth we will get free. It is only we haven't experienced the truth. I may theoretically know the truth but if I don't experience God's nearness in a concrete way, I may still have doubts or be unsure. Many of us are not free to enjoy God simply because we haven't experienced him. I am in disagreement with the old saying of, "we don't rely on feelings, only faith." I believe it is both. There are times when I simply need to trust by faith and there are times I need to experience something concrete. Often in our theology we swing too far one way, usually you will find though the truth is closer to the middle.[71] In my God pursuit I have always craved the manifest presence of God. I want to FEEL God. I am not ashamed of this. I am in a relationship, I'm supposed to feel something. God has honoured my desire and I have had countless experiences with God in my walk with him, from quiet peace-filled moments to loud, burning, dramatic ones. I don't dictate to God how he wants to touch me but I freely let him come. He knows what I need.

I know many of us are disappointed because we don't experience God the way we want. I don't want to try to explain why it goes like this, only to say I have had my own disappointments but I have refused to give up on God. My strong will/stubbornness has been an asset to me in this regard. Yes, sometimes I let go and sort of 'give up' but after some time I get frustrated and my passion rises again,

"God I want you, I love you." I choose to worship in spite of my disappointment. God promises he will answer us.

And without faith it is impossible to please God, because anyone who comes to him must believe that he exists and that he rewards those who earnestly seek him. Hebrews 11:6

God rewards me with himself.

---

[70] This is the same greek work as earlier ginōskō, to know by use of the five senses, an experiential knowing.
[71] I'd like to credit Rick Joyner. He has a wise understanding of many spiritual things and says the path of life is most often found in the middle between two extremes. For example, if lawlessness is on one side, legalism is on the other.

After this, the word of the Lord came to Abram in a vision: "Do not be afraid, Abram. I am your shield, your very great reward." Genesis 15:1

Healing the great divide of matter and spirit means understanding I am one with God through Jesus Christ. We are one already. I do not go through religious loop holes or rituals to ascend, I have already ascended.

And God raised us up with Christ and seated us with him in the heavenly realms in Christ Jesus...Ephesians 1:6

Christ has already descended. What is happening now is in all things I do, it is for the purpose of being concious of the truth. It is the renewing of my mind.

For who knows a person's thoughts except their own spirit within them? In the same way no one knows the thoughts of God except the Spirit of God. What we have received is not the spirit of the world, but the Spirit who is from God, so that we may understand what God has freely given us. This is what we speak, not in words taught us by human wisdom but in words taught by the Spirit, explaining spiritual realities with Spirit-taught words. The person without the Spirit does not accept the things that come from the Spirit of God but considers them foolishness, and cannot understand them because they are discerned only through the Spirit. The person with the Spirit makes judgments about all things, but such a person is not subject to merely human judgments, for, "Who has known the mind of the Lord so as to instruct him?" But we have the mind of Christ. 1 Corinthians 2:11-16

I have the mind of Christ. What I must learn is how to access his mind. My own mind is full of noise and its own thoughts. What Christians call "spiritual disciplines" are in reality, there to give us tools to hear, feel and align to the mind of Christ, to let my own mind be re-aligned or transformed to his mind. Spiritual disciplines help us to receive from God, they are not there to please God or satisfy religious requirements. This is not a takeover, but a conscious and freely made decision to come into union with Jesus. These disciplines can include; scripture reading, worship through music, arts or silence, prayer by words or journalling, acts of service or ministry in an organised setting or meeting, fasting, walking in nature and more. All of these things help me to become aware of God, his heart, his ways, and his thoughts. They do not however bring me closer to him, they can and do however make me aware of him. See the difference? I would recommend the classic literature *The practice of the presence of God* by the 17th century monk Brother Lawrence to flesh out this whole topic. It deserves more thought and contemplation than what I'm giving it here and others have written important books on this topic including *The Supernatural Power of a Transformed Mind* by Bill Johnson.

The Father is not looking for us to prove ourselves with discipline or church attendance or religious activity.

He has shown you, O mortal, what is good. And what does the Lord require of you? To act justly and to love mercy and to walk humbly with your God. Micah 6:8

Religion that God our Father accepts as pure and faultless is this: to look after orphans and widows in their distress and to keep oneself from being polluted by the world. James 1:27

Primarily we don't have a 'religion'.[72] We have a relationship. The current understanding of the word and practice of religion is tied to the 1300 to 1500's in England and having a system of faith and allegiance to a higher power/powers however Online Etymology Dictionary says this of the root meaning of the word, "However, popular etymology among the later ancients (Servius, Lactantius, Augustine) and the interpretation of many modern writers connects it with religare "to bind fast" (see rely), via the notion of "place an obligation on," or "bond between humans and gods."[73] Yes Christianity is a religion with rituals and structures but these are centered relationally not organisationally. We bind fast to God! I like this understanding of religion.

---

[72] The word religion is mentioned only five times in the New Testament scriptures and not once in the Old Testament.
[73] https://www.etymonline.com/search?q=religion. Accessed 23rd January 2024

The fruit of this relationship will be; time spent with God in spiritual practices because we want to be with him, serving and ministering in church because we love the family of God, volunteering with the poor and underprivileged because we care about righteousness and justice. This relationship unites spirit and matter, it unites heaven and earth, and it unites all that is separated. The very word 'religion' for me does not define my union with God. It means different things to different people depending on our experiences. For some it is a dirty word, due to abuse or control experienced, for others it is comforting, offering cultural identity and social inclusiveness. Religion for me is not something I practice, nor is it something I need to belong to humanity. However, spirituality would more accurately describe my adventure with God and a living connection to a supernatural being. I do not desire a form or structure but substance and this substance is love. Love that holds everything together, love I cannot escape from. As I sit here typing I breathe in love, I breathe in God. Love fills every cell in my body, love fills me as I sit on the toilet. Love fills me as I'm intimate with my husband. Sometimes Holy Spirit speaks to me while I'm on the toilet or while I'm with my husband. There is no place where God is not.

Where can I go from your Spirit? Where can I flee from your presence? If I go up to the heavens, you are there; if I make my bed in the depths, you are there. If I rise on the wings of the dawn, if I settle on the far side of the sea, even there your hand will guide me, your right hand will hold me fast. If I say, "Surely the darkness will hide me and the light become night around me," even the darkness will not be dark to you; the night will shine like the day, for darkness is as light to you. Psalm 139:7-12

Even in the dark places God is there, in our dark sinful moments. God may be grieved by our dark things, he may weep and his face be turned away like a parent who can't bear to look when his child has been badly injured. But God is still right there with us in our dark places. His light wants to break in and have us walk in the light as he is in the light. God sees our heart, he does not judge by appearances.

The Lord does not look at the things people look at. People look at the outward appearance, but the Lord looks at the heart." 1 Samuel 16:7

Our parent God knows who we truly are, what our deepest desires are. He sees past the walls, the bandages, the self-medication in all its forms to numb the pain. He sees gold, he sees his very own image. In our journey with God as we allow her to, she will take us on an adventure into our own heart, to find her image. We were made to shine the brightness of God in all its glory. Yes it's true God does not share his glory with another.[74] But if we allow the process of being transformed, we are not another, we are becoming one with God. This became reality when Christ bridged the gap between us and God and between spirit and matter. There is no separation on any level.

For me to become one with God I become love. Everything that is not love in me must be taken away. Often in our Christians circles we talk about being stripped or we say we must die daily and carry our cross. This is true but could it mean more than what we have currently understood? Let's read from Mathew,

Then Jesus said to his disciples, "Whoever wants to be my disciple must deny themselves and take up their cross and follow me. For whoever wants to save their life[75] will lose it, but whoever loses their life[76] for me will find it. Mathew 16:24-25

This word life in the greek is psychē and it can be translated as life or soul. Look at the very next verse where psychē is used again, but this time the translators have chosen to use the word soul,

What good will it be for someone to gain the whole world, yet forfeit their soul? Or what can anyone give in exchange for their soul? Mathew 16:26

---

[74] See Isaiah 42:8 "I am the Lord; that is my name! I will not yield my glory to another or my praise to idols."
[75] Underlined for emphasis
[76] Underlined for emphasis

To be consistent in translating, what if we placed the word soul in Mathew 16:24-25? It would then be, *For whoever wants to save their soul will lose it, but whoever loses their soul for me will find it.*

This changes the way we might interpret these well-known verses. I want to credit the late John Paul Jackson for introducing me to this concept. What if Jesus wants our soul to die and for us to 'lose' our soul in order for us to find our soul in Christ? Could it not be that instead of the usual concept we have that we must "die",[77] or as we have often interpreted it, repress our own life/desire, that instead, we allow our soul to be exposed to Jesus. We lose our soul to him so he can take it, inspect it and change it to become more like his. This then would be the very opposite of the current, common understanding. I do not repress and cover up my soul and whip it to death but I offer it uncovered to Christ to take and allow him to do with it as he wishes. Then I will find life in him. I call this the grand uncovering. Wow, this is becoming something glorious, but not very easy.

---

[77] I'm not discounting physical death or the value of one who has been martyred for Christ. Let us honour those who followed Jesus as he called them this way. Martyrdom for some was and is a "cross they carry." Also, can it be these verses are talking about more than just receiving life after physical death?

CHAPTER 9

The Grand Uncovering

The next season of my life took me by surprise. Instead of finding a job in journalism after graduating from the one year course, I had a burning desire to attend another school, situated in a beautiful coastal city less then one hour from where I had studied. This was a Christian leadership training school with an international youth ministry. It did not make sense in the natural but I couldn't shake the urge to go. The money did not come so easily this time and I had to be patient. In the end, the last of the money needed was given after the school started. The school was short, only three months long. I did however meet some amazing local leaders and people. The youth ministry organised outreach events for youth. Two key leaders I met were youth pastors in a local church, who were also serving within the international ministry. It is here I felt I should stay and serve. My next mission was to find a job, it was tough and I started out cleaning elderly and disabled people's homes.

It was right at this point the international directors of the youth ministry asked if I wanted to become a missionary in the ministry and move to the U.S.A to be a part of the community there. They felt I was in need of a stronger team around me. My heart leapt within me. This was it. This was what I had been waiting for. I was to become an official missionary in a modern youth movement. Yet as I walked along the beach, I heard my Father's voice.

"You don't belong to (name of the ministry). You belong to me." I was upset. I wanted to be a part of something bigger than myself. I felt lonely at times. I longed for structure and something concrete around me and stable people who were traveling the same road. God seemed to be jealous. With difficulty, I needed to go back to the international directors and tell them I wouldn't be going to America and I would stay serving voluntarily where I was. In this particular ministry, people raise support money as income. I am not sure the leaders understood my decision however they were honourable, if I felt I had heard from God then what could they do. It was a big thing to turn down the offer, like something got taken away from me...again. Was it always going to be this difficult?

In the middle of the uncertainty and a job that didn't provide enough hours, I eventually felt led to give my Curriculum Vitae to a local cafe/ restaurant who hired me despite me having no experience in that field of work. This was a wonderful place to work and I learned a lot about myself. I'm not naturally a tactile or physically orientated person yet this work was. I learned to overcome some doubts about myself and improve my skills. My boss was wonderfully understanding and never yelled at me even when I dropped a tray of hot drinks. In the busy weekends she would put me on counter to serve the customers, recognizing my people skills. I am forever grateful to the wonderful couple who employed me at this time. Father gave me to them to serve and although they didn't claim they were "christians" I had a lot of respect for them and viewed them as his. In all this, God was continuing to dismantle "unholy duality" in me.

Something in me died after I had said no to moving to America. I was restless and filled with uncertainty. What was I doing? Things didn't make sense. Although I felt a certain joy that God was jealous of me and I had the freedom to keep going with him the way I was used to. I couldn't put the puzzle pieces together. It seemed as though I was jumping from one thing to another without a clear sense of direction. I had fully offered myself to God and I felt as though I were dying. A dear friend in this season gave me some quotes from Thomas Merton, which in essence said when we are harsh on ourselves by our own act of will rather than by the sword of grace given by Holy Spirit then our soul will take revenge by being cruel to itself and to others. This is what a false ascetic does.

However, if we wield the sword of God's grace and will on ourselves through the leading of the Holy Spirit; this is the "meek" violence[78] which Jesus refers to in the kingdom of Heaven.

This explained so much. I had been violent with myself repeatedly in the past and had suffered anger and bitterness. I was hard towards others primarily because I was hard on myself. The heart of God for me and us is that as his will comes to pierce us, we do indeed die, our soul, our passions die but this is for the purpose of receiving true peace and become "hidden with Christ in God." This happens as we offer ourselves to him, not as we crush ourselves.

The blade of God's will was piercing my heart as I choose to stay in New Zealand and remain where I was, working as a barista in a cafe. I did experience a dying and as I look back on my journal notes I see a shift in my relationship with God. Life was coming. Father is kind, in that season I met three women whose influence on me remains to this day. I would not be who I am without them.

These strong, women warriors understood me and like me wanted to swim in the deep things of the Spirit. In that season they were like water wings, buoyancy aids keeping me afloat. I was not alone after all. Father did give me the support I needed, on his terms.

The blade of his will was about to be thrust deeper. At this point in time I had a "goth" identity. I dyed my hair dark and wore clothes that were "edgy". Anything pink or frilly disgusted me and I prided myself on my "strong" look.

I watched a lot of television revolving around the supernatural. These programmes often came on late at night (before the era of Netflix) and I remember it was about midnight and I was alone in the house, sitting

---

[78] See Mathew 11:12

on my couch watching the opening credits for the show. Suddenly, I became paralyzed. Two bright blue eyes were staring at me. I froze, the fear of the Lord came upon me, He was watching me, like really! I sensed him say I was not to watch the programme because I was going after the wrong kind of supernatural and I was to give up my cherished external identity. These were hindering me from receiving from God what he wanted to give. I'm not saying we can't watch supernatural things or wear what we want but for me, they were now obstructions. Having the fear of the Lord is not something I **do** but the fear of the Lord **is a Spirit**, the Lord himself. Holy Spirit as I perceived her, with her blue eyes, was piercing my soul.[79]

And there shall come forth a rod out of the stem of Jesse, and a Branch shall grow out of his roots: And the spirit of the LORD shall rest upon him, the spirit of wisdom and understanding, the spirit of counsel and might, the spirit of knowledge and of the fear of the LORD. Isaiah 11:1- 2

These verses speak about Jesus. The spirit is the Holy Spirit who here is described as having seven facets; the spirit of the Lord, the spirit of wisdom, understanding, counsel, might, knowledge and the fear of the Lord. This sevenfold description of the Holy Spirt is found also in Revelation 3:1 and Zechariah 3:1-10 which references again the branch (Christ) and describes him as a stone with seven eyes. The sevenfold Holy Spirit is much like the Trinity; something we find difficult to explain, seven but one.

Let's remember the definition of sinning — to miss the mark. God had come to me again to examine my heart and help me not miss the mark for my life because I desired the best. I didn't want the good, I wanted the best, I wanted him. I was willing to continue to allow him to test me. Abraham went through this.[80] Jesus went through this when he was led by the Spirit into the desert to be tested.[81] I wanted more, I wanted to go deeper.

[79] I'm not saying the Holy Spirit has blue eyes. I believe God takes any form she wishes to communicate with us in the way we need.
[80] See Genesis 22:1-12
[81] See Mathew 4

The fear of the Lord leads to life; then one rests content, untouched by trouble. Proverbs 19:23

The promises of God as we surrender everything include true peace, contentment and being untouched by trouble. Not that external trouble doesn't come to us but our inner life is unmoved and stays anchored in a child-like trust in God. What an antidote to the epidemic of anxiety plaguing us.

The fruit of the Holy Spirit becomes visible in us, love, joy, peace...etc.[82] These are not something we manufacture but are of genuine substance and experience, the characteristics of God himself abiding in our being as our soul absorbs his nature. It is possible to live in perfect peace within oneself, the exterior world may be in chaos but the interior world in quiet and trust.

This is what the Sovereign Lord, the Holy One of Israel, says: "In repentance and rest is your salvation, in quietness and trust is your strength, but you would have none of it. Isaiah 30:15

As the above verse indicates, this is a choice. Will we surrender, will we give up our soul to find life? My choice in this season meant turning to God to give me the supernatural things I craved and allow God to take from me my covering. You see I was hiding behind my image. My "goth" image made me feel strong and powerful. God perceived my heart and knew the motivation behind my choice. If I dress how I wish for freedom and expression this is one thing, if I dress to protect myself from my own insecurities this is entirely different. This is not freedom, I am being controlled by my own brokenness. I truly understand the need to protect oneself. Father is not judging us. Now however God was offering me the invitation to allow him to be my covering instead of sewing my own fig leaves together.

Then the eyes of both of them were opened, and they realized they were naked; so they sewed fig leaves together and made coverings for themselves. Genesis 3:7

---

[82] See Galatians 5:22

We have been constructing our own coverings since the beginning. In most cultures of course we wear external coverings, likewise we tend to wear coverings for our inner self as well. These are different for every person. My coverings for my inner self were yes, giving me a sense of protection but on the flip side shielding me from receiving what my inner self needed. And more importantly preventing me from union with God, for there was something between us. As I transitioned and let my hair grow and be its natural colour and as I put away some of the more extreme items of clothing and accessories, I did literally feel naked. It was terrible, alongside feeling naked, I felt invisible. I was now small, common and brown, like a sparrow, these are the terms in which I thought of myself. I could be crushed or stepped on anytime. These were of course lies and they needed to be exposed. My good Father wanted me to believe the truth about myself, but he had to strip the facade away to reveal what was underneath. We needed to go deeper still to find his image in me, to the truth of him calling me good and being made in his image. My petite frame, white skin, blue eyes, light brown hair and biologically feminine gender were good. More than good in his sight, I am perfect.

I am a visual person, perhaps more so than most. One of the best ways I learn is visually and I am extremely imaginative. I see many things in my mind. Having a striking image has always been something I value and to put away what I thought was a strong image was difficult. What kind of image would I have now? Would I have an image at all? We are, in our wealthy, western world a visual generation, since we do not struggle to find our daily food and we have adequate shelter and our basic needs met, we can care about how we appear and create beauty around us. This is good. God loves beauty, look at creation. He gave us the job of being caretakers of the entire planet.[83] I really enjoy the way my generation does care about the environment. This is righteous, this is God in us.

[83] See Genesis 1:28

So our Father has nothing bad to say about our freedom to cultivate an image or celebrate beauty. What he is concerned about is if this intrudes upon our relationship with him. Something became exposed with startling clarity. I despised weakness. More honestly, I hated my own weakness. I felt physically weak and I thought I looked weak. Being 158 centimeters (5.2 feet) and forty something kilograms means I am on the small side of things. As an adult, I felt tall people were taken more seriously, they had "physical stature." And I was a girl, girls were "weaker" than boys. There was even a scripture backing up that thought.[84] In the middle of this exposure Holy Spirit led me to these verses,

The Sovereign LORD has given me a well-instructed tongue, to know the word that sustains the weary. He wakens me morning by morning, wakens my ear to listen like one being instructed. The Sovereign LORD has opened my ears; I have not been rebellious, I have not turned away. I offered my back to those who beat me, my cheeks to those who pulled out my beard; I did not hide my face from mocking and spitting. Because the Sovereign LORD helps me, I will not be disgraced. Therefore have I set my face like flint, and I know I will not be put to shame. He who vindicates me is near. Who then will bring charges against me? Let us face each other! Who is my accuser? Let him confront me! It is the Sovereign LORD who helps me. Who will condemn me? They will all wear out like a garment; the moths will eat them up. Who among you fears the LORD and obeys the word of his servant? Let the one who walks in the dark, who has no light, trust in the name of the LORD and rely on their God. Isaiah 50:4-10

There is a direct correlation between submitting fully to God and allowing him to instruct you and him becoming the one who will help and vindicate you. In this new season, rebellion was to be put away and I was to offer myself to God and people even if they might beat or mock me. Brother Yun in his book The Heavenly Man[85] says the hurtful words he received in Western countries

---

[84] See 1 Peter 3:7. There are various interpretations of what this verse means which I'm not going to address here. You see my point in referencing this, I was perceiving the "weakness" as bad and feeling as though scripture 'backed' this up.
[85] The Heavenly Man by Brother Yun and Paul Hattaway published 2003

were more painful than the physical beatings and torture he experienced in China. I needed to uncover myself. In this, I would become someone who has a word for the weary and I would not be put to shame, God would help me.

This directly confronted me and my need to be strong, my fear was that I could be beaten or mocked and I have no way to defend myself. I had a memory from high school where I sat down in the class and a tall male classmate came and told me to, "get off, that is my chair." I remember thinking I couldn't have fought him or defended myself against him physically, he was stronger.

This moment defined my internal dialogue, it was bad to be a petite girl.

In this uncovering process, Holy Spirit led me to an important understanding. All of us must come to him, the good and the bad. He wants to take it all. Look at these verses from Colossians one,

The Son is the image of the invisible God, the firstborn over all creation. For in him all things were created: things in heaven and on earth, visible and invisible, whether thrones or powers or rulers or authorities; all things have been created through him and for him. He is before all things, and in him all things hold together. And he is the head of the body, the church; he is the beginning and the firstborn from among the dead, so that in everything he might have the supremacy. For God was pleased to have all his fullness dwell in him, and through him to reconcile to himself all things, whether things on earth or things in heaven, by making peace through his blood, shed on the cross. Once you were alienated from God and were enemies in your minds because of your evil behavior. But now he has reconciled you by Christ's physical <u>body through death to present you holy in his sight, without blemish and free from accusation</u>[86]—if you continue in your faith, established and firm, and do not move from the hope held out in the gospel...Colossians 1:15-23

We must be presented to God, in this presentation the blood of Jesus removes all darkness. I am holy but for me to know I am holy the sin and brokenness must come to the light.

[86] Underlined for emphasis

If I leave some part of me covered, how can I receive Jesus into those parts and how can accusation be removed from me? It is our own accusing voice that condemns us and the enemy happily joins in and echoes what we are already thinking. My crap, my darkness MUST come to God. God wants it, he welcomes it, he is longing to have it all so we can have his all. We become light as he is light, we become holy as he is holy. Nothing is hidden from him.

Nothing in all creation is hidden from God's sight. Everything is uncovered and laid bare before the eyes of him to whom we must give account. Hebrew 4:13

However, I must choose to present to him the parts I think are unpresentable. As I choose to do this, the blood of Jesus flows, life flows and my mind receives life, every accusation is silenced as I understand the truth of the great exchange, his life for mine, mine for his. He absorbs my sin and death is swallowed up in victory. I absorb life. This is the great exchange, this is why we lean in to our beloved for we are receiving so much more than we are able to give and this is perfect. God first loved us. He is the great lover. A good lover will not force someone to uncover themselves, a true lover waits for the beloved to willingly do so. Just as God is waiting for some of us to come, if all we have is brokenness then this is what he wants. It is for my benefit to be laid bare for I return to the original condition I was made to have, union with God. In this union, nothing separates us. This is the mystery Paul brings revelation to quoting Genesis 2:24,

"For this reason a man will leave his father and mother and be united to his wife, and the two will become one flesh." This is a profound mystery—but I am talking about Christ and the church. Ephesians 5:31-32

Union between a man and woman is a picture of something greater, Christ's union with his church. My uncovering is to bring me unashamed to Christ where he shares all he is with me as I share all I am with him. I cannot bring a fake me, or a me I construct for myself. What person wants to be with a false image of someone? We all long for authenticity in the other, the real person. My deepest desire was and is to be one with God. All of this was leading me to my greatest hope. In spite of the anguish, I felt and the feeling as though my chest were being ripped open, I allowed myself to go through the process. Fear was making way for love.

CHAPTER 10

Return to innocence

In the book *The voyage of the Dawn Treader* by C.S Lewis, we meet Eustace a boy who is under a spell and has been changed into a dragon. Eustace up until now has been grumpy, demanding and self-centered. He found a dead dragon's treasure trove and through his pride and lust becomes bound to it and is morphed into a dragon. Eustace feels sad and lonely, isolated from the rest of the group. He goes off by himself and encounters the lion- Aslan (a Christ figure) who leads him to a bubbling well with marble steps going down into it. As Eustace gazes into the water, it occurs to him that as snakes peel off their skins so he could too. Eustace begins scratching at his scales and his whole skin peels off. Except shortly thereafter his skin becomes once again hard and scaly and he proceeds to scratch again at this scales. He does this three times with no effect on his scaly skin.

Aslan tells him that he must undress him and Aslan begins to tear at him with his claws. Eustace is transformed into a boy again after Aslan takes off his skin and Eustace swims in the pool.[87]

In our soul surrender to Jesus, trying to heal and remove our own "skin" will not work. Only as we follow Jesus will he lead us to healing pools and remove our "scaly skin" for us. As I experienced and like Eustace, my dragon self-showed me how sad and lonely I really was. We have spent so long trying to protect ourselves and guard our treasure we don't realise our true state. I was sad and lonely.

[87] From The Voyage of the Dawn Treader by C.S Lewis. 1952

In fact, for the years prior many people had prayed for the "loneliness" they sensed in me but nothing changed. We would like to think if someone discerns something and prays for us then it will suddenly get better. Often though these issues are deep within us, unconsciously there by our own choice and cannot be "prayed away." We are a new creation and we are BECOMING a new creation. Jesus takes us on the journey "further up and further in".[88] This takes time and work.

Following Jesus is not a passive state. It means taking up our cross and allowing our soul to be crucified. The cross was heavy. Remember though the promise of life. We do not stay in this continual cross bearing state, we die and are resurrected to greater glory. I don't believe it is only about being resurrected bodily, although this will happen but a resurrection of our true self in this life.

Now if we are children, then we are heirs—heirs of God and co-heirs with Christ, if indeed we share in his sufferings in order that we may also share in his glory. Romans 8:17

Jesus shares our life and we share his, he is our big brother and is continually praying[89] for us.

Both the one who makes people holy and those who are made holy are of the same family. So Jesus is not ashamed to call them brothers and sisters. Hebrews 2:11

In the middle of this stripping, I felt discouraged. Was I really hearing from God? To my amazement as I visited my home church in the city I grew up in, two special men prayed for me. They repeated word for word the sentence I felt I had heard God say to me, I was being built line upon line, precept upon precept, they even quoted from Isaiah 50:4-10 about my ears being opened to hear God. They prayed endurance for me, for even youth get tired and weary and said I had been flying straight like an arrow and on track with God even if it seemed jumpy and disjointed to others.

---

[88] Paraphrased from C.S Lewis The Last Battle 1956
[89] See Romans 8:34

They prayed some other things over me concerning my destiny and the future. What an encouragement this all was and it fanned hope in me to persevere. God loves to encourage us, he knows when we need it. I was young then and still in infancy in my ability to hear and understand God's voice. It is much easier for me these days and I don't need so much affirmation and confirmation from people in my walk. Sometimes I still ask him to confirm things, to write this book I asked for confirmation and someone came to me saying they saw me with a pen writing heavenly words. We are never too far along to need others however in our youth whether we are speaking biologically or spiritually we are in need of greater emotional support. If you are young in God, be it physical age and/or spiritual age do not be ashamed to ask for help. Expect God to comfort you, expect him to confirm things, he DOES answer.

A key word these lovely men gave me which was important was this, become Son conscious, not sin or self-conscious, a confidence that rests in Jesus; not self-confidence but Son-confidence. This is a powerful word and one I share because it's true for all of us. In our surrender to Christ who is our life, we move from focusing on self to focusing on him. This changes everything. Religion is really good at making it about us. I'm good or I'm bad. I did this or I haven't done that. However as we gaze on him, he becomes the centre. I am neither good nor bad but I am in him. Just as God revealed himself to Moses, he proclaimed himself to be I AM.

Moses said to God, "Suppose I go to the Israelites and say to them, 'The God of your fathers has sent me to you,' and they ask me, 'What is his name?' Then what shall I tell them?" God said to Moses, "I AM WHO I AM. This is what you are to say to the Israelites: 'I AM has sent me to you.' " Exodus 3:13-14[90]

Since we are made in God's image we too bear this name "I am" We are not the great I AM but we have the same DNA as our Creator. Our identity does not need anything attached to it for us to be complete.

[90] I AM also can be translated I WILL BE WHAT I WILL BE

Because we exist, we are complete. We have no need to prove anything or do something. We are. This is amazing and relieving. My whole being as it rests in the knowledge of I am, can focus on Jesus. It is not that I become less or swallowed up, it is that I am freed from self. I do not need to worry about myself because I am like him.

Dear friends, now we are children of God, and what we will be has not yet been made known. But we know that when Christ appears, we shall be like him, for we shall see him as he is. 1 John 3:2

Think of young children, they are. They are not constantly self-reflecting or wondering what their place is or if they have done enough or not done enough. Nor do they overtly concern themselves with their appearance or compare themselves to others. They are innocent; this is the condition God wants us all to have, innocence. This is part of what it means to return to the tree of life instead of eating from the tree of the knowledge of good and evil.

Innocent ones need protection, like sheep that need a shepherd to guard against predators. God likens us to sheep,

We all, like sheep, have gone astray, each of us has turned to our own way; and the LORD has laid on him the iniquity of us all. Isaiah 53:6

Jesus comes as the good shepherd to lay down his life for the sheep. He said,

"I am the good shepherd. The good shepherd lays down his life for the sheep. John 10:11

I have often been offended we are likened to sheep. Aren't sheep quite stupid? They follow one another without thinking, even to their own death. Of all the animals we had to be like sheep. This is not how God thinks. The most worshipped and worthy one in scripture is Christ the Lamb.

Then I saw a Lamb, looking as if it had been slain, standing at the center of the throne, encircled by the four living creatures and the elders. The Lamb had seven horns and seven eyes, which are the seven spirits of God sent out into all the earth. And when he had taken it, the four living creatures and the twenty-four elders fell down before the Lamb. Each one had a harp and they were holding golden bowls full of incense, which are the prayers of God's people. In a loud voice they were saying: "Worthy is the Lamb, who was slain, to receive power and wealth and wisdom and strength and honor and glory and praise!" Then I heard every creature in heaven and on earth and under the earth and on the sea, and all that is in them, saying: "To him who sits on the throne and to the Lamb be praise and honor and glory and power, for ever and ever!" Revelation 5:6-13

The lamb, one of the most innocent and gentle creatures is the symbol or the way God, the Son of Man wants to represent himself. The all powerful, almighty, all knowing Creator of the entire cosmos chooses to represent himself as a lamb and not only that he goes to his death as a lamb, slaughtered for us.

He was oppressed and afflicted, yet he did not open his mouth; he was led like a lamb to the slaughter, and as a sheep before its shearers is silent, so he did not open his mouth. Isaiah 53:7

In my uncovering season, Holy Spirit said this,

"Jenna, surrender to the Lamb, you can surrender to the Lion but can you surrender to the Lamb?" I was horrified at the implications. I knew exactly what Holy Spirit was getting at. In all my walk with God, I had revered the Lion, the Jesus with the burning eyes and the sword coming out of his mouth. I had needed him to be my strong protecter, I had needed his justice and fierceness. I reveled in throwing myself into the mane of the lion, like Lucy does with Aslan.[91] I was afraid of the Lamb. The lamb is defenseless. What attributes did the lamb have that I valued? The lamb frolics; is cute, gentle and sweet. I did not like or identify with any of this. One time at the age of sixteen a boy gave me a little stuffed toy and told me I was cute, I remember being offended. I wasn't cute, I didn't want to be cute. Could I not be something else? Beautiful or glamorous or noble or strong? Anything but cute or delicate or sweet.

---

[91] This scene is found in the book The Lion, the Witch and the Wardrobe by C.S Lewis 1950

I did not reject what Holy Spirit said to me but I was pained. Now what? Was my whole identity going to be dismantled? Did I really have to become a sweet, silly little thing?

However, I did not yet grasp the deeper meaning. It is exactly the nature of the lamb that dismantled death and darkness. The nature of the Lamb is the most powerful force in the universe, even as I write I am weeping. This beautiful pure One who did nothing wrong, full of gentleness and humility who went about only doing good, healing the sick, casting out demons and speaking life to the people. This Lamb allowed himself to be beaten, stripped and crucified so his blood would flow for us. We are the ground beneath that bloody cross, we who are made from earth receive this sacred blood to give us life and heal us.

But he was pierced for our transgressions, he was crushed for our iniquities; the punishment that brought us peace was on him, and by his wounds we are healed. Isaiah 53:5

This world reveres the strong, the invincible. The bold and beautiful are idolised as are those who can cut others down with their words or win in sport against weaker opponents. We celebrate war and use force to take dominion over people and whole nations. Conquest and conqueror, these are normal for us. Behind all this there is the presupposition that we must take what we want and by force if necessary. In our daily lives it lies lurking beneath the surface; climb the ladder in your workplace, earn more money at the expense of others. Consume what you wish even if this means some people live below the poverty line. We shut our eyes to the big picture. I do too. It is more convenient and beneficial for me to buy a cheap product from my local chain store than to try to source something ethically and sustainably produced. Yes, I try sometimes but then I fall back into what is easiest for me. I applaud those of you who make consistent efforts to be conscious of the bigger picture and not only focus on your little world. It seems we are all in the grip of a "fight to survive" mentality, a global one. This self-centeredness strangles us and not only us but the whole of creation and it goes all the way back, look at this account of the first two brothers,

Adam made love to his wife Eve, and she became pregnant and gave birth to Cain. She said, "With the help of the LORD I have brought forth a man." Later she gave birth to his brother Abel. Now Abel kept flocks, and Cain worked the soil. In the course of time Cain brought some of the fruits of the soil as an offering to the LORD. And Abel also brought an offering—fat portions from some of the firstborn of his flock. The LORD looked with favor on Abel and his offering, but on Cain and his offering he did not look with favor. So Cain was very angry, and his face was downcast. Then the LORD said to Cain, "Why are you angry? Why is your face downcast? If you do what is right, will you not be accepted? But if you do not do what is right, sin is crouching at your door; it desires to have you, but you must rule over it." Now Cain said to his brother Abel, "Let's go out to the field." While they were in the field, Cain attacked his brother Abel and killed him. Genesis 4:1-8

Cain killed his own brother in a jealous rage. We continue to kill our own brothers and sisters when we covet, desire and do not get what we want, literally and spiritually.

Then the LORD said to Cain, "Where is your brother Abel?" "I don't know," he replied. "Am I my brother's keeper?" The LORD said, "What have you done? Listen! Your brother's blood cries out to me from the ground. Genesis 4:9-10

When Jesus died as the Lamb, he spoke to Abel's injustice, his blood still speaks to all the injustice done through self-centeredness.

...to Jesus the mediator of a new covenant, and to the sprinkled blood that speaks a better word than the blood of Abel. Hebrews 12:24

Jesus's blood covers us and frees us from self-centeredness. To become the Lamb means I receive a humble and gentle heart, an innocent heart which will not be violent towards another and use force to get my own way. Instead,

I allow God to vindicate me if I am wronged and entrust myself to the one who will raise me from the dead. As I humble myself, I will be exalted.

Humble yourselves, therefore, under God's mighty hand, that he may lift you up in due time. Cast all your anxiety on him because he cares for you. 1 Peter 5:6-7

You can see here the reason we find it difficult to be humble, we have anxiety related to who will care for us. This is rooted in what *Fatherheart Ministries* calls an orphan spirit.[92] An orphan is left to take care of themselves and so enters into the "fight for survival" mentality. Pride is involved, it takes humility to allow someone to be bigger than us and fear is involved, fear the other person will hurt me if I surrender myself to them. The character of God the Lamb is absolutely trustworthy. This is what causes me to weep, this is the reason I entrust myself to God the Lamb. Fear is banished, pride flees as I look upon the one who for love gave up his life for mine. This is a God I will serve. This is the magnificent beauty of the good news about Jesus Christ. We have heard so much theology and religious teaching yet at the centre there is one thing upon which all else is built upon and around which the entire universe rotates, Christ crucified.

For you know that it was not with perishable things such as silver or gold that you were redeemed from the empty way of life handed down to you from your ancestors, but with the precious <u>blood of Christ, a lamb without blemish or defect. He was chosen before the creation of the world,</u>[93] but was revealed in these last times for your sake. 1 Peter 1:18-20

Jesus the lamb was never an afterthought. He was the plan all along.

...the Lamb who was slain from the creation of the world. Revelation 13:8

Everything in God's history with people is and was to lead us into this revelation. The heart of a Creator-lamb who loves us.

---

[92] I would recommend their resources. More information for Fatherheart Ministries can be found at https:// www.
fatherheart.net/
[93] Underlined for emphasis

The progression of revelation is always moving. At each step in human history as revealed in scripture we move closer to the heart of God. God chose the nation of Israel to begin with, yet God's intention was never that we would camp around a temple or be afraid of his presence. In Christ we would see the fulfillment of God's heart to be united in love with people who would freely choose him and be just as in love and passionate with him as he is about them. Each generation freely chooses God for themselves and we have the privilege of being in this age, the age of the kingdom where we have full access without fear to the heart of God. Paul writes,

But I am afraid that just as Eve was deceived by the serpent's cunning, your minds may somehow be led astray from your sincere and pure devotion to Christ. 2 Corinthians 11:3

It was Christ who came to walk with Adam and Eve in the Garden,

Then the man and his wife heard the sound of the LORD God as he was walking in the garden in the cool of the day, and they hid from the LORD God among the trees of the garden. Genesis 3:8

I would like to mention and give credit to Michael Fickess for pointing this out but "in the cool of the day" is not quite an accurate translation. The Hebrew here is ruach yown which is literally, in the breath, wind or spirit of the day. So, the presence of God came and Adam and Eve hid. From the beginning we were meant to be in God's presence, naked and unashamed. Our glory was the breath of Holy Spirit, our life was in Christ the tree of life, our care was in the hands of Father God. And then our minds were led astray. Our innocence rests in returning to God, trusting in the Lamb to remove our stained conscience by pouring his blood over our minds. The way is open. We want to walk in your breath again God, we want to come in joyful celebration to you, innocent and free.

You have not come to a mountain that can be touched and that is burning with fire; to darkness, gloom and storm; to a trumpet blast or to such a voice speaking words that those who heard it begged that no further word be spoken

to them, because they could not bear what was commanded: "If even an animal touches the mountain, it must be stoned to death." The sight was so terrifying that Moses said, "I am trembling with fear." But you have come to Mount Zion, to the city of the living God, the heavenly Jerusalem. You have come to thousands upon thousands of angels in joyful assembly, to the church of the firstborn, whose names are written in heaven. You have come to God, the Judge of all, to the spirits of the righteous made perfect, to Jesus the mediator of a new covenant, and to the sprinkled blood that speaks a better word than the blood of Abel. Hebrews 12:18-24

Just as Adam and Eve walked in the breath of God, so too can we. At pentecost, the breath of God came back to us,[94]

Suddenly a sound like the blowing of a violent wind came from heaven and filled the whole house where they were sitting. Acts 2:2

Restoration had begun!

---

[94] Michael Fickess teaches this restoration of God's breath

CHAPTER 11

Through the narrow door into expansion

"*M*any today are spending and being spent in work for Jesus Christ but they do not walk with him. The one thing God keeps us to steadily is that we may be one with Jesus Christ. After sanctification, the discipline of your spiritual life is along this line. If God gives a clear and empathetic realisation to your soul of what he wants, do not try to keep yourself in that relationship by any particular method but live a natural life of absolute dependence on Jesus Christ. Never try to live the life with God on any other line than God's line and that line is absolute devotion to him. The certainty that I do not know—that is the secret of going with Jesus.*"[95] *Oswald Chambers.*

In my dying, a new way was opening. My dearest mentor had a picture of me, I was lying flat on the floor as though dead but then I became a river, flowing out and flowing onwards. She said my desire was good and as I pondered my desire it crystallised into one thing. I wanted God. Yet there was no pattern of formula to which I could hold to. Years earlier I had heard Holy Spirit say this to me,

"It is more than a pattern, more than a formula. It is a life-time commitment to the deep working love of Christ Jesus all the days of our lives, to follow him." Just as Oswald Chambers writes above, it is about living a life of natural dependence. Spiritual disciplines are not the goal, Jesus is the goal. Being surrounded and immersed in all things Christian is not the goal, living life as a light, being the light of Christ in this beautiful world is where the life is.

[95] Quoted from My UPMOST for His Highest by Oswald Chambers, first published 1927.

The prevalent dualistic mentality enforces the idea of us squeezing our way through life and trying to avoid 'worldly contamination.' Many use this scripture to back this idea,

Do not love the world or anything in the world. If anyone loves the world, love for the Father is not in them. For everything in the world—the lust of the flesh, the lust of the eyes, and the pride of life—comes not from the Father but from the world. The world and its desires pass away, but whoever does the will of God lives forever. 1 John 2:15-17

John here is talking about the spirit of the world. Just as it says,

As for you, you were dead in your transgressions and sins, in which you used to live when you followed the ways of this world and of the ruler of the kingdom of the air, the spirit who is now at work in those who are disobedient. Ephesians 2:1-2

The ways of the world and the spirit of the world are what John is referring to. He is not saying we cannot love people in the world or the "world itself" meaning creation in its entirety or art or music or any other glorious thing God has given us to enjoy. It is the spirit behind something we must pay attention to. As Paul writes,

The acts of the flesh are obvious: sexual immorality, impurity and debauchery; idolatry and witchcraft; hatred, discord, jealousy, fits of rage, selfish ambition, dissensions, factions and envy; drunkenness, orgies, and the like. I warn you, as I did before, that those who live like this will not inherit the kingdom of God. But the fruit of the Spirit is love, joy, peace, forbearance, kindness, goodness, faithfulness, gentleness and self-control. Against such things there is no law. Those who belong to Christ Jesus have crucified the flesh with its passions and desires. Galatians 5:19- 24

The flesh is different from the soul. Let's remember when Paul uses the word flesh he uses it as an opposite to spirit. As we live by the Spirit: our will, soul and body will surrender to align to the Spirit. In this place we are free to enjoy life. This is one reason we are given the Holy Spirit, he leads us in this new way of living as we are born again and become God's children. The flesh will join to the ruler of this world but our spirit joins to Holy Spirit. These are our two options.

We know that anyone born of God does not continue to sin; the One who was born of God keeps them safe, and the evil one cannot harm them. We know that we are children of God, and that the whole world is under the control of the evil one. 1 John 5:18-19

In the above scripture, it says, **"the One who is born of God"**, this is Jesus and he truly does keep us safe. As we live in this material world we are spiritually safe. I say spiritually safe because we cannot deny that sometimes our bodies are exposed to danger or are hurt or become ill. This does not negate the truth we are promised that we are safe from the evil one. We are free to explore this world in confidence, we have been delivered from evil. I can go anywhere with absolute assurance no evil power can harm me. Darren Wilson the Christian film maker portrays this beautifully in his films, especially *Furious Love*[96] and *Father of Lights*[97]. Look at this verse,

Do not be afraid of those who kill the body but cannot kill the soul. Rather, be afraid of the One who can destroy both soul and body in hell. Mathew 10:28

I used to think the "One" here was talking about the devil and then one day I understood it was talking about God! This showed me how fearful I was and how I attributed too much power to the evil one. God and the devil are not having a boxing match. The enemy is not an equal opponent to God. The evil one is a created being who rebelled against God and was displaced from his position in heaven.[98] Since the crucifixion and resurrection of Jesus Christ the enemy has been disarmed.

And having disarmed the powers and authorities, he made a public spectacle of them, triumphing over them by the cross. Colossians 2:15

---

[96] Furious Love Written and directed by Darren Wilson© Wanderlust Productions 2010
[97] Father of Lights Written and directed by Darren Wilson© Wanderlust Productions 2012
[98] See Isaiah 14, this chapter may be speaking of this event.

The dictionary defines disarm as; Take a weapon or weapons away from and deprive of the power to hurt. As I enter into crucifixion and resurrection with Jesus, the enemy's power over me is disarmed. The only way he can have power over me is if I give it to him. Jesus is the way to the Father, he is the gate. He is the one who gives us safety and life.

I am the gate; whoever enters through me will be saved. [99] *They will come in and go out, and find pasture. The thief comes only to steal and kill and destroy; I have come that they may have life, and have it to the full. John 10:9-10*

Have life to the full! This is glorious, yet we often feel as though we walk a tightrope or we are not really free, we may feel as though we walk a narrow road.

"Enter through the <u>narrow gate</u>[100]. For wide is the gate and broad is the road that leads to destruction, and many enter through it. But small is the gate and <u>narrow the road that leads to life</u>[101], and only a few find it." Mathew 7:13-14

Look at the underlined parts above, it says narrow **gate** and narrow the road that **leads** to life. It does not say the way is narrow after we have entered in. In fact, when we go in, we find pasture and abundant life. What does pasture look like? Jesus is describing himself as narrow because he is the only way to the Father.[102] It doesn't mean Jesus stays narrow. Jesus said,

He said to them, "Go into all the <u>world</u>[103] and <u>preach</u>[104] the gospel to all creation. Mark 16:15

Here he was speaking to his eleven disciples and it is a mandate for us also as the twelve disciples were instructed to tell all followers of Jesus to obey everything he had commanded them to.[105]

---

[99] This is the greek word sōzō and in the strong's dictionary means, to save, i.e. deliver or protect (literally or figuratively):—heal, preserve, save (self), do well, be (make) whole.
[100] Underlined for emphasis
[101] Underlined for emphasis
[102] See John 14:6
[103] Underlined for emphasis
[104] Underlined for emphasis
[105] See Mathew 28:20

The word world in the greek is *kosmos* and is used to denote the following: *government, the stars, the universe, the earth, the human race, world affairs, earthly goods which included endowments and riches and finally the gentiles as contrasted to the jews, in other words, all people groups.* The word preach in the greek is *kērysso* and is defined as *to herald (as a public crier), especially divine truth (the gospel):—preacher(-er), proclaim, publish.* The dictionary defines the verb herald as, *Be a sign that (something) is about to happen.*

We go out as a sign into all the cosmos with the beautiful news of the new kingdom. This doesn't seem like a narrow road. It is an invitation to join in the expansion of the new kingdom. A kingdom of love where the Lamb rules. It was time to be released from limitations. In my continued process of moving from death to life, I needed to understand the endurance and perseverance required.

We do not want you to become lazy, but to imitate those who through faith and patience inherit what has been promised. Hebrews 6:12

I had faith and was full of fire but did I have patience? Not understanding the call to be a sign in the cosmos will undermine our sense of purpose and will feed into the escapism mentality. I needed this encouragement from *The Torch and the Sword* a book by Rick Joyner,

"The fire burns but what you lack is discipline and endurance. You walk adequately for short periods. Now you must learn to walk with endurance. You must resolve to walk each day in the domain over which the Lord has given you to rule. He has given you authority but you must walk with him in your domain. Only then will you be fruitful and multiply as you are called. Your domain is your garden. The path of life always leads to unity and harmony—with God first, and then with all that is his. This takes strength and endurance because the whole creation is now in discord and opposes unity."[106]

[106] The Torch and the Sword by Rick Joyner© 2003 MorningStar Publications.

Jesus says this to Rick,

"You will know these chosen ones by the fire that already burns in them. They will never be content with religious practices, for they yearn for me and the reality of this realm. Because they seek me I will be found by them. I will give them their heart's desire–my fellowship. I will be their inheritance."[107]

Many think of fire solely as a symbol of judgement. However John the Baptist said this,

John answered them all, "I baptize you with water. But one who is more powerful than I will come, the straps of whose sandals I am not worthy to untie. He will baptize you with the Holy Spirit and fire. Luke 3:16

And then look what happened when the Holy Spirit came,

They saw what seemed to be tongues of fire that separated and came to rest on each of them. Acts 2:3

Fire also represents the presence of God. In the Judaic temple, the lampstand stood in the holy place. The lampstand represents Christ[108]. The Priests were instructed to never let the lampstand go out and it was to be continually tended.[109] As we come into union with Jesus we burn as he burns, we become light, we become fire. For a fire to keep burning, it needs heat, oxygen and fuel. Jesus is our high priest who gives us these things, it is he who ignites our fire and gives his love, his breath. He is our fuel our: bread, water, wine and honey. He pours the oil over us.[110] Yet to receive these things we must come to him and even more, learn to live IN him. Our coming to him consistently means we learn HOW to live in him. It is new for us to learn to live by the Spirit. It could be likened to us who cannot naturally breath underwater being transformed and learning how to breath underwater. What was once unnatural becomes natural. So it is with us as we learn to live by the Spirit.

---

[107] The Torch and the Sword by Rick Joyner© 2003 MorningStar Publications.
[108] Everything in the temple and about the temple was a 'shadow or copy of things to come, literally Christ himself, see Hebrews 7-8 and Colossians 2
[109] See Exodus 27:20-21
[110] We can find all these 'fuel' metaphors within scripture

As I learnt to live in this way, everything became spirit. As we have discussed, in Christ there is no separation between matter and spirit. I will never forget the morning I woke with God telling me to listen to the song *Release Me* performed by the band Pearl Jam. This was incredible to me as I heard my Father's voice in the lyrics of the song. God declared my identity to me saying I was like him, and how I have "opened up". I was in awe of this life affirming message considering the difficult process I had been in. I was simultaneously ecstatic that he would choose to use a Pearl Jam song for this. The world is wide open for us as we live in the Spirit.

...one God and Father of all, who is over all and through all and in all. Ephesians 4:6

It is exciting to live in the wide open spaces with him. A few months later I got the opportunity to go to the Rainbow Gathering in the U.S.A. This gathering is a huge new age festival, no money is allowed and everything is given and shared. Our team went to feed people and share the love of Jesus. I am not a particularly practical person and this was quite some experience. There were no showers, you had to dig your own toilets, find wood for fires, etc. I did wonder what I was doing there but was encouraged when the group leader asked me what I saw in the spirit and I understood my place better. However, the stand-out point for me came as I pondered why I couldn't "cross the line". By this I meant why I couldn't do crazy and mighty exploits for God and see his power released in tangible ways. God's answer to me was this,

"Remain in my love, the time is not right for me to place you in what I have been preparing you for. My love casts out all fear."

Father is more interested in our well-being than in what we can do for him. It is wild in the wide open spaces and any good parent wants their child to be given access to things when they are ready and will be able to handle themselves and not get hurt. It is the same in our relationship with

God. As our inner capacity is expanded so will our outer capacity expand. We can of course run ahead, and may well find ourselves in trouble if we do. There is this old saying in charismatic christian circles, "Girl's/Guy's, gold and glory." In other words these are the things likely to cause us to stumble or fall. It is our emptiness which drives us to seek illicit sexual encounter[111], money or the wrong kind of adoration from people. As God's love fills our being the emptiness dissipates. It is not that we need to "control" ourselves it is rather we become satisfied with God and have no desire to pursue those other things. Self-control is a fruit of the spirit and *The Passion Translation*[112] bible translates this fruit as "strength of spirit".[113] The root word in the greek means power, dominion, strength and might. Strength comes to us by the Holy Spirit and is not based on our will but by him filling our hearts. My longing to do something for God was good but not if it was outside of my capacity to handle it. Trusting God involves accepting his wisdom for us even when it seems counter-intuitive. John the Baptist said this,

"A person can receive only what is given them from heaven." John 3:27

John said this in answer to his disciples when they expressed dismay because everybody was going to Jesus instead of John. It is not for us to decide "our ministry". It is given to us from heaven. Quite frankly this is and was relieving. I knew too well the cost of going outside my assigned influence and in social media speech; #burnout, #let'snotdothatagain, #staysafewithinyourborders. I was a little disappointed though, I couldn't deny my desire to see some big action. On my return home, I needed to channel my energy somewhere and put it into organising prayer meetings with youth. In spite of the expansion in my inner world, the outer world remained limited. I was learning the tools necessary to safely navigate the great cosmos waiting for me to explore. We can become discouraged if we look at others and what they are doing and compare ourselves.

---

[111] I am in no means referring to normal and healthy sexuality expressed within proper boundaries

[112] The Passion Translation®. Copyright © 2017, 2018 by Passion & Fire Ministries, Inc. Used by permission. All rights reserved. ThePassionTranslation.com.

[113] See Galatians 5:23 TPT

We must learn to look only at the eyes of love and not compare ourselves at all.

We do not dare to classify or compare ourselves with some who commend themselves. When they measure themselves by themselves and compare themselves with themselves, they are not wise. We, however, will not boast beyond proper limits, but will confine our boasting to the sphere of service God himself has assigned to us, a sphere that also includes you. 2 Corinthians 10:12-13

We are all made unique with different skills, talents and life experiences. Those who have faced great difficulty and pain are given grace accordingly as Father the wise judge knows exactly their capacity. Those who have been given more in life will be held responsible for what they received. This is justice. We are not treated equally, we are treated with equity. Consider this parable Jesus told,

"Again, it will be like a man going on a journey, who called his servants and entrusted his wealth to them. To one he gave five bags of gold, to another two bags, and to another one bag, each according to his ability. Then he went on his journey. The man who had received five bags of gold went at once and put his money to work and gained five bags more. So also, the one with two bags of gold gained two more. But the man who had received one bag went off, dug a hole in the ground and hid his master's money. "After a long time the master of those servants returned and settled accounts with them. The man who had received five bags of gold brought the other five. 'Master,' he said, 'you entrusted me with five bags of gold. See, I have gained five more.' "His master replied, 'Well done, good and faithful servant! You have been faithful with a few things; I will put you in charge of many things. Come and share your master's happiness!' "The man with two bags of gold also came. 'Master,' he said, 'you entrusted me with two bags of gold; see, I have gained two more.' "His master replied, 'Well done, good and faithful servant! You have been faithful with a few things; I will put you in charge of many things. Come and share your master's happiness!' "Then the man

who had received one bag of gold came. 'Master,' he said, 'I knew that you are a hard man, harvesting where you have not sown and gathering where you have not scattered seed. So I was afraid and went out and hid your gold in the ground. See, here is what belongs to you.' "His master replied, 'You wicked, lazy servant! So you knew that I harvest where I have not sown and gather where I have not scattered seed? Well then, you should have put my money on deposit with the bankers, so that when I returned I would have received it back with interest." 'So take the bag of gold from him and give it to the one who has ten bags. For whoever has will be given more, and they will have an abundance. Whoever does not have, even what they have will be taken from them. And throw that worthless servant outside, into the darkness, where there will be weeping and gnashing of teeth.' Mathew 25:14-30

Notice, not everyone was given the same amount and were therefore not expected to use beyond what they had and were given the same reward. The one who thought his master was a hard man had a distorted view of him and his fear crippled him from taking action. Fear will rob us and this fear comes from not understanding who God really is. The image we create in our thinking will manifest into reality. This may sound like a hard truth yet we have so much more authority than what we currently use. We are made in the image of God after all. We can trust Holy Spirit to lead us into truth if we are willing. For some of us, it is a matter of determining what we have been given. Start with the little you have, this is all that is required. For me it was serving the local youth through prayer and being faithful to my employees and getting my driver's license. (I was confronting fear in me as I did this) I began to feel God's pleasure in me as I learnt discipline and setting small goals and achieving them. Jason Upton a worship leader tells a story about a bass player he played with who had a T-shirt that said, "God loves you but I'm his favourite" I began to feel the truth of this. I was living in a small world in my little beach town but the growth and love in my heart was exploding. I too was the big expanse God's love was being poured into. In this season I wrote this,

I cry out, a rending, a tearing.

Head thrown back, arms out.

My chest is ripped open, a new heart, a heart of flesh.

A new beat, on my knees panting, gasping.

Fresh wind is blowing and I'm learning how to breath.

CHAPTER 12

The quiet dark of trust

I laughed gloriously like a child. The grass tickled my back and the sun stroked my face. All prior thoughts flew away. I soaked in the Son, his light soothing my soul. Father carried me on his back, we could go anywhere together, and even better, we were always together. It was New-Year's-day 2006 and I was at a monastery called The Star of the Sea, situated in a high place overlooking the sea. I had gone there to receive my battle plans for the year. All day I waited,

"Father what is the plan this year?" The scenery was gorgeous and the monastery a quiet place of tranquility where the presence of God hung in the air like a curtain softly blowing in the breeze. I didn't see or feel either of these as I trudged around in my combat boots waiting for my instructions. As the day rolled into late afternoon I sighed in exasperation and went and sat on a bench at the back of the monastery. The sea lay before me an open expanse. The sun glistening off the water and grass of the hill seemed to herald the loveliness of God in a quiet and unassuming manner. I heard Holy Spirit,

"Roll down the hill." What! Was I hearing things?

"Roll down the hill." And so in a clumsy thump to the ground and with some anxiousness I rolled over the bumpy grass my arms and legs everywhere, the hill was steep enough to gather quite some speed. What a sight this 25-year-old must have been rolling down the hill but what I found bursting from me were child-like screams of delight. It was exhilarating. I had not done anything like this in years, preferring the peace of keeping myself upright on solid ground. As I hit the bottom still laughing deliriously and letting myself recover from the spin Holy Spirit said,

"This is the battle plan." Oh the joy that filled my heart. I didn't fully understand, yet something in my spirit did. And the great weight of "adult" responsibility lifted from me. I hadn't realised I had picked up the weight. I was the kind of person to swing from one extreme to another and since God had been leading me into consistency and focus, I had gone too far one way and been giving into the "striving squeeze". It's like when we try too hard in something and our face screws up and we can't breath. Well, Father let the unholy air out of this huffing, puffing balloon and filled me with the lightness of himself. Sometimes we become so bound up in the frantic pace of daily life, we haven't realised we dropped our joy along the way. Children live in this space of joy, they play with delight and allow those bigger than themselves to give guidance, instruction and provision. In the meantime they play happily, fully immersed in the joy of the moment. This was what God wanted for me. Not in my wildest dreams had I expected this. Life was becoming a beautiful thing, not something to be endured but something to be enjoyed. And so it was on another shiny day a few weeks later as I was walking home from work and listening to Jason Upton's song *The Cost of Intimacy*, Jesus came to me and thrust a sword in my soul, I literally doubled over in the street. I recognised he was separating me to himself and was separating between my soul and spirit.

For the word[114] of God is alive and active. Sharper than any double-edged sword, it penetrates even to dividing soul and spirit, joints and marrow; it judges the thoughts and attitudes of the heart. Hebrews 4:12

Jesus, the word and sword of God, was in a last prophetic act finalising the process I had been in. I remember it was the most relieving and painful sensation. As I continued walking and worshipping out on the street, I felt the breath of life flowing over me in waves, I truly was breathing new air.

Following this a little time later I had another encounter I will never forget.

---

[114] Underlined for emphasis. This in greek is logos. Which John uses for Christ in John 1.

It was though Holy Spirit manifested in my room, blue waves of light or what could have been hair in an almost human like but obscured form. I couldn't tell if she was male or female. I heard,

"Your eyes will grow dark and you will not see where you are going, you will have to trust me and I will lead you." Holy Spirit was telling me my prophetic vision was going to be darkened (in other words not function and I would have to trust her without "knowing" what was coming). I had become good at seeing into my future or at least understanding what was happening in my life. But what did this mean now? I wasn't afraid, only wondering.

There is one thing I have come to understand in my journey with God; real trust is about letting go of control. Real love is forged in the fires of trust. To go deeper means trust and I was about to be plunged in deeper than I had imagined. Around the same time I also felt God was asking me to give up my rebellious sense of privacy. I am rather private by nature and am selective with what I share and when. People think I am open, the reality is I choose to be open. I will remain closed if I feel I'm in an unsafe space and the person/people or situation will not honour my openness or pay the attention I feel I/it deserves. I am picky like this. To some extent we all should be like this and not give our "pearls to the pigs" but there is a line where we can take our privacy too far and actually shut out life by our unwillingness to take a risk. I wrote in my diary,

What more do you want of me Lord and you say ALL. And I scream and I bleed, I resist, I call on death and you are rather wanting to silence my cry, lift me from my bloodied state and raise me to life in you. SURRENDER. I will not choose death, I choose life.

So the plan now was, roll down hills and not know where I am going! LOL[115], sounds brilliant for letting go of control and trusting. When God is silent about something, we wait and trust.

[115] Abbreviation for Laugh Out Loud.

In some christian traditions there is something called, "The dark night of the Soul". This is in reference to a place in God where it is dark and one feels cut off from him, one may suffer depression and go through periods of unbelief and suffering. John of the Cross [1542-1591] a Spanish mystic, Roman Catholic saint, Carmelite friar and priest wrote a poem upon which this based, yet he didn't call it the Dark night of **the Soul** but only *The Dark Night* and look at what he calls the night, *"in darkness and secure"* and *"Oh that glad night."* He found security and was glad in the dark;

1.   One dark night,
fired with love's urgent longings
—   ah, the sheer grace! — I went out unseen,
my house being now all stilled.
2.   In darkness, and secure,
by the secret ladder, disguised,
—   ah, the sheer grace! —
in darkness and concealment, my house being now all stilled.
3.   On that glad night,
in secret, for no one saw me, nor did I look at anything, with no other light or guide
than the one that burned in my heart.
4.   This guided me
more surely than the light of noon to where he was awaiting me
—   him I knew so well —
there in a place where no one appeared.
5.   O guiding night!
O night more lovely than the dawn!
O night that has united
the Lover with his beloved, transforming the beloved in her Lover.
6.   Upon my flowering breast which I kept wholly for him alone, there he lay sleeping,
and I caressing him

there in a breeze from the fanning cedars.

7.   When the breeze blew from the turret, as I parted his hair,
it wounded my neck with its gentle hand,
suspending all my senses.

8.   I abandoned and forgot myself, laying my face on my Beloved;
all things ceased; I went out from myself, leaving my cares
forgotten among the lilies.[116]

Darkness is not necessarily a bad thing,

If I say, "Surely the darkness will hide me and the light become night around
me," even the darkness will not be dark to you; the night will shine like the day,
for darkness is as light to you. Psalm 139:11-12

The unborn are hidden in the dark of the womb, seeds are buried in the
dark of the ground, night itself is temporal waiting for the sun to rise again.
Hope remains in these dark places and hope does not disappoint us. Yes hope
deferred can make us sick,

Hope deferred makes the heart sick, but a longing fulfilled is a tree of life.
Proverbs 13:12

Christ in us is our hope[117] This beloved poem speaks of the divine union,
St John writes in verse 8, *I went out from myself, leaving my cares...* The night
is a place where we "leave ourself". It is not a denying of self but a turning
from self to give to another. True love is mutual giving and receiving. In our
broken world we often get stuck in the death and sorrow. The true purpose
of this poem I believe was not to express or explain the journey of suffering
or depression[118] but rather to call us into union with the beloved.

[116] Licensed by Creative Commons.
[117] See Colossians 1:27
[118] Physical trials or sufferings I believe may be excluded in this context.

It is a call for courage to face the dark night and be willing to go in to find our Love. In my heart of passion, I find it difficult to believe that Father leaves us in a "Dark night of the soul" to suffer without experiencing his presence, it may be I don't "feel" him there but he is there, he promised he wouldn't leave me and as I trust he is there I can come into greater peace.

There are beautiful people in history who say they went through years of anguish enduring the "Dark night of the Soul" and I am not desiring to minimise their experience. Yet a passionate cry rises within me, we are called to be in constant communion with the one we love, what kind of relationship is it if the one we are married to stops communicating with us for 30 years? Depressed is surely what I would be. Remember what we believe is powerful and will create our reality.

What did the dark of quiet trust bring? Within the next year and a half, I met my husband, got married and moved to a new country. Imagine if I would have foreseen that? I would have freaked out. The Father does not withhold things from us, he protects us. Sometimes this means protecting us from ourselves. I was still learning how to overcome in life and I still had bouts of exhaustion. My emotions were not what I could call stable and this was obvious as I began my relationship later that year with my now husband. When we enter a season of quiet trust it is for our benefit. I have a prophetic story I must re-count from this time before the life-changing events. Life shifted quickly in my personal life after my blue-haired Holy Spirit encounter. I had been living in a gorgeous house we named the princess palace with open views towards the sea. Living with us was a young 15-year-old who we were fostering although I had taken the main responsibility for her. (Which was done with all love and sincerity in my heart but I still had trouble taking responsibility for myself at times, not so much in terms of outward responsibility. I paid my bills, cleaned, cooked and went to work consistently but it was with my emotional and mental well-being) Within a few months I had moved house and lived as a boarder, our foster girl had moved to a home in another city and I was suddenly relieved of responsibility except to take care of myself. As I walked on a wild beach in New Zealand to get some God space, my employers had taken us away for a weekend retreat, I felt the Holy Spirit tell me to,

"Pick up that rock." I thought that was weird since there were thousands of rocks lying on the stony beach, I couldn't shake the impression and so I put the rock into my jacket pocket without giving it a second thought. Some days later as I was in my room I thought about the rock in my jacket pocket. I had been looking at my moonstone, an egg-shaped stone which is pale blue and has a reddish light inside if held against the light. I relished my moonstone. It was given to me by a dear friend and symbolised my journey in the supernatural things of God. As I held the dark grey rock, I gasped, it was the exact size and shape as my moonstone and had a white indent on one side, it looked like the rock had a scar. In my spirit I felt the Holy Spirit say this was the natural realm and I need to cherish and embrace this realm also. I love to have tactile things around me as symbols of what God is saying and these two rocks remind me of God's lessons for me. I still have them.

It was Easter time and I reflected in my journal the following;

He (Jesus) is my rear guard, He is all around me. I felt him tell me,

"Don't ever think I'm not carrying you. Learn all you can from the mentors I've placed in your life but hold on to what I have taught you. You are called to hold on to the end of my train. Don't stop now. Wait on me. This is your endurance, your maturity."

Fire thoughts, fires need to be built up. They need the right foundation and beginning. They need attention to detail, care and time. Sometimes the embers are glowing and the fire is hot but it is not dramatic with flames. The fire still burns, although it may appear as though it has gone out. This is us sometimes.

I picked up a rock, an earth rock, symbolising my intent to remain on earth, my commitment to this world. To EMBRACE MY HUMANITY. It lies next to my moonstone, the spiritual or supernatural realm. Both are realities. Christ is our reality; fully divine and fully man. Natural and supernatural. They are not in conflict with each other. Jesus was not in conflict with himself. He was not fragmented, He understood truth.

Son of Earth
Son of Man
Son of God
God

My to-be husband had arrived the month prior from Finland for the leadership course I had done with the youth ministry two years earlier. We hosted a party for our international guests and I found myself sitting on my couch overlooking the sea talking to a fascinating person. I feel as though I am looking down a deep, dark well not knowing if I will reach the bottom. It is from this moment a divine spark is ignited. Both of us wanted to push the other away, we had our own reasons but the Father had other ideas and through a series of God interventions, including a romantic walk in the moonlight followed by hot chocolate near midnight in my work cafe, we couldn't deny the pull toward the other. The evening of our "God date" I had gone to one of my mentor's house to confess my attraction to this man so I would have someone to talk to about it after he left and try to keep living my life. As I was walking home back from her house a figure came towards me in the dark, No, it can't be him! What was he doing here? I stopped short in front of him and in a girlish tone I had never used before said the most clever thing,

"What are you doing here?" Not that he told me that evening, but he had actually gone to my house and circled it, wondering if he should knock at my door. He had decided against it and there we were pulled together in the dark anyhow. I still laugh thinking about it. That season of entering into our relationship was tumultuous for me. My sense of equilibrium disappeared as did my feeling of safety. I couldn't believe the "good" being offered to me and it was even harder to think Father was giving me a gift of a beautiful husband. I wanted to run. I said to my husband at that time,

"I'm not able to live life with a white picket fence." My metaphor for what I considered a mundane go-to-work, day-to-day, two point two kids life. I had my plans, I wanted to to go a supernatural school in Canada. I wanted the reality of God, I wanted his fireworks. I was afraid I would be blocked in my pursuit of God if I married. I remember my husband laughed when I forcefully said it. He wasn't put off at all. Thankfully he enjoyed my fire and he has wise eyes to see. I've never met a person more capable of "seeing" someone than him. He was the first guy I had met who I felt really "saw" me. And the most "non-religious" person with a true faith I had met who understood me, a winning combination. The lovely lady whose house I was boarding in was a pivotal person in helping me overcome my fear about this relationship. She encouraged me to "be friends" with him and invite him out. (She had had a dream of us getting married. She was wise enough to keep that information from me) God had again put me around me the right people to guide me. I am constantly amazed at his ability to do this, the condition being I chose to listen to him telling me where to go and be if he does so. I was on a rollercoaster of a ride that included visiting Finland two months later to find out who this person was and what this was all about. He had planned to come back to New Zealand again the next year. It was too much for me, my impatience put me on that plane and I was officially, according to him a "crazy monkey." I had felt prompted to give him my moonstone before he left not knowing if I would see him or the moonstone ever again. I mourned. He got the supernatural rock and I was stuck with the ugly earth one. This highlights the great importance of this season for me, truly allowing the two realms to become intertwined. We had not made concrete promises to each other and the uncertainty of it all was hard to bear. I could make some very good movies scenes from some of my moments in this period. I couldn't eat, it was hard to sleep, my skin broke out and my body actually manifested irregular hormonal behaviour. I had fallen hard, straight onto the earth from my previous floating in the air. The shizz was getting real.

This season was about living and trusting. God truly isn't looking for sacrifice. He is looking for a heart to love him and others. Yes, I knew what sacrifice was, in my following him I had "sacrificed". Can you really call it sacrifice though when it means gaining your true heart's desire? It may feel like it is in the beginning and then you discover it wasn't a sacrifice after all as your true heart's desire flourishes. In the whirlwind of all this I tried my best to remain focused on letting go. Even after my ten weeks spent in Finland getting to know this mysterious man, we still made no concrete promises and I was left hanging in the balance. Talk about learning trust. Our trust is not in people or in things, it is in God.

Some trust in chariots and some in horses, but we trust in the name of the LORD our God. Psalm 20:7

My own expectations even about God were confronted and this quote from the book *Disappointment with God* by Philip Yancey spoke straight to my heart and consolidated all I had been learning,

"Why doesn't God intervene and make himself obvious? Why doesn't he speak aloud so we can hear him? We yearn for miracle, for the supernatural in its pure unadulterated form. I chose the word 'unadulterated' deliberately because it portrays a sentiment that is central to this issue. We moderns strive to separate natural from supernatural. The natural world that we can touch and see and smell and hear seems self-evident; the supernatural world however is another matter, there is nothing certain about it, no skin on it and that bothers us. We want proof. We want the supernatural to enter the natural world in a way that retains the glow, that leaves scorch marks that rattles the eardrums. The God revealed in the bible does not seem to share our desire. Whereas we cleave natural from supernatural and seen from unseen, God seeks to bring the two together. His goal one might say, is to rescue the "lower" world to restore the natural realm of creation to its original state, where spirit and matter dwelt together in harmony.[119]

Going deeper with God means rooting out presuppositions we have, things we "expect" from God. In essence it means learning to love him in return unconditionally. Yes, he could snap his fingers and move the world for me but do I love him for what he can do for me or because of who he is? This is maturing love. To love God with no strings attached, what a pleasure it must be for him. It is like when Jesus said to his disciples,

I no longer call you servants, because a servant does not know his master's business. Instead, I have called you friends, for everything that I learned from my Father I have made known to you. John 15:15

In these later years, this verse from scripture moves my heart,

Jesus replied, "Foxes have dens and birds have nests, but the Son of Man has no place to lay his head." Mathew 8:20

---

[119] Disappointment with God by Philip Yancey. Marshall Pickering publications ©1998

I want to be the place where Jesus can lay his head. For this to happen I need to be relaxed and be without demands and questions. Can any of us rest when there is someone demanding something from us or asking questions, or expecting something. God wants to find a resting place in us. Christ is the head of the church and we are his body. We are the temple where he dwells.

Instead, speaking the truth in love, we will grow to become in every respect the mature body of him who is the head, that is, Christ. From him the whole body, joined and held together by every supporting ligament, grows and builds itself up in love, as each part does its work. Ephesians 4:15-16

In him the whole building is joined together and rises to become a holy temple in the Lord. And in him you too are being built together to become a dwelling in which God lives by his Spirit.

Ephesians 2:21-22

Look at this verse from Jeremiah,

...The LORD will create a new thing on earth — the woman will <u>return</u>[120] to the man." Jeremiah 31:22

The word translated here as return comes from the root word *cabab* which means to *revolve, surround, or border.* Different bible translations have also rendered this word as *surround, encompass, embrace, shelter and protect.* I believe not only is this verse speaking of the restoration of females to a place of equality but also as a reference to Christ and the church. We the bride embrace Christ. We become his place of shelter. This is incredible. I have been delving deeply into this, I encourage you to find out what this means for you too.

Trust is essential to find rest. God rests on us and in us as we learn to trust him. Modern psychology says, "The most important aspect of trust in close relationships appears to be faith: the belief that one's partner will act in a loving and caring way whatever the future holds."[121]

[120] Underlined for emphasis
[121] Rempel, Holmes and Zanna, 1985 https://psycnet.apa.org/record/1985-30794-001

Whatever the future holds, will I trust God even when he appears to be silent about something? Trust frees us from worry to live each day with joy in our hearts. Consider the words of Jesus,

Therefore do not worry about tomorrow, for tomorrow will worry about itself. Each day has enough trouble of its own. Mathew 6:34

I have learnt (mostly) to let God worry about things for me. Recently I had some medical procedures which I didn't want. I said to God,

"If you want me to be stuck with needles and go through this, It's your problem. It's your responsibility to take care of me, this body is yours. You know what you have planned and what you want me to do." It's the same with sickness. If I am due to speak somewhere and I get sick and cannot go, it's on God's shoulders. He is the one taking care of me. This may sound arrogant but it is the opposite. I entrust myself to him. He is looking to be the responsible one, it's his job as the parent. I am freed from fighting for myself. I am freed from the survival mentality. This is how Paul and Silas could sing worship songs after being beaten and thrown in prison. I don't believe they were trying to be brave warriors, I believe they were trusting in God to do with them as he wished. They were spiritually and literally in the quiet dark of trust.

The crowd joined in the attack against Paul and Silas, and the magistrates ordered them to be stripped and beaten with rods. After they had been severely flogged, they were thrown into prison, and the jailer was commanded to guard them carefully. When he received these orders, he put them in the inner cell and fastened their feet in the stocks. About midnight Paul and Silas were praying and singing hymns to God, and the other prisoners were listening to them.

Suddenly there was such a violent earthquake that the foundations of the prison were shaken. At once all the prison doors flew open, and everyone's chains came loose. Acts 16:22-26

Look what happened as these two men turned their hearts to God in spite of the pain and the dark, the prison doors flew open and **everyone's chains**

came loose! When we are set free to live in an inner place of trust, others are set free. The chains binding others become loose. The atmosphere of trust we create enables others to come into greater freedom. What a way to shine our light in this world. The same rain may be falling on us all and we have an entirely different response, a trusting and peaceful response. This is the way of being a child of God. This is what all of creation is groaning for,

I consider that our present sufferings are not worth comparing with the glory that will be revealed in us. For the creation waits in eager expectation for the children of God to be revealed. Romans 8:18-19

Our sufferings are nothing compared to the glory "growing within us." The whole of the cosmos is looking to us to be the herald of peace, to be a sign of trust in the ever-growing confusion and uncertainty. The fullness of Christ in us is being as the Prince of peace is.[122] And so we willingly come to the dark night, as St John beautifully wrote,

3.   On that glad night,
in secret, for no one saw me, nor did I look at anything,
<u>with no other light or guide</u>
<u>than the one that burned in my heart.</u>[123]
4.   This guided me
more surely than the light of noon
<u>to where he was awaiting me</u>[124]
—   him I knew so well —
there in a place where no one appeared.
5.   O guiding night!
O night more lovely than the dawn!
<u>O night that has united</u>
<u>the Lover with his beloved,</u>
<u>transforming the beloved in her Lover.</u>[125]

[122] See Isaiah 9: 6 for Christ's title of Prince of Peace
[123] Underlined for emphasis
[124] Underlined for emphasis
[125] Underlined for emphasis

With no other light or guide than the one that burns in our hearts let us go to where he is awaiting us, the night of being united to our Lover and being transformed in Him. To the quiet dark of trust we will go, knowing he is there, knowing a far greater glory is being worked out in us. Help us not to be afraid Jesus, we come to you.

CHAPTER 13

Life on the Mountain

At the beginning of the trust season a precious spirit sister said to me, "Jenna, ask God for your name." She spoke in reference to this verse,

Whoever has ears, let them hear what the Spirit says to the churches. To the one who is victorious, I will give some of the hidden manna. I will also give that person a white stone with a new name written on it, known only to the one who receives it. Revelation 2:17

Scripture is multi-layered, yes this verse is speaking of a time to come and to a specific church however as we have been discussing, time is not a linear line from God's point of view and Holy Spirit can take a verse and breath life on it for the one who has ears to hear. I did ask God for my name but I did not expect his reply, nor the way in which he spoke it to me. I am sitting in the movie theatre, Father Christmas is on the screen handing out presents to the Pevensie children.[126] As Lucy receives her present Father Christmas says,

"The juice of a fireflower, one drop will heal any injury." I immediately hear,

"That is your name, you are a fireflower." The presence of Holy Spirit surrounds me and tears run down my cheeks. I am Fireflower. It made perfect sense. I see myself planted on a high mountain, my face turned to the Sun/Son basking in the warmth and light. This little flower with her whole being open to the radiance of Jesus, is safe and happy in a high place. In my awakening to the Spirit, I had experienced the fire burning on me many times. My back and head would burn. I would feel his love pouring over me. Red had been a prominent colour for me.

126 Taken from a scene in a movie adaptation produced by Walden Media 2005 titled The Chronicles of Narnia: The Lion, the Witch and the Wardrobe based on C.S Lewis's book The Lion the Witch and the Wardrobe.

Holy Spirit told me to buy a shiny, bright red duvet cover. As I slept under it, I felt protected by Jesus's blood and fire. In colour psychology red is known to help overcome depression. It is a vivacious, bold, life-giving colour. I needed red in my life. The one on the throne is described as having the appearance of jasper and ruby.

And the one who sat there had the appearance of jasper and ruby. A rainbow that shone like an emerald encircled the throne. Revelation 4:3

There was no strategy for me to execute except be planted on the mountain and burn. I was tested. On New Years day after my husband had an important encounter for him which conformed to him our being together, he phoned me asking if I would marry him. This may sound strange but in the early days of our friendship I would burn when he was around me, the presence of Holy Spirit would manifest. Right before he asked me the question, my chest began to burn and I knew what he was about to ask. I could say yes without hesitating. I had moved to the capital city and was about to begin a new job. My fiancee packed up his life and moved to New Zealand, we got married later that year. Right on Hebrew New Year, something I had not previously paid attention to, my husband found out he had won an art competition. It was necessary for him to go back to Finland for an extended period of time and oversee the project. Holy Spirit said to me,

"You are starting a new life in Finland." And so, I was newly married and being sent to the opposite side of the world. I did not know what awaited me and was excited for the adventure. I had no understanding of what it is to move to a completely different country where a different language is spoken. I did not foresee the difficulties I would face and the way in which I was affected. We have words to describe this phenomena:culture shock. We arrived in Finland in December the beginning of winter. We couldn't live in my husband's rental for another half year due to a pre-signed contract. We stayed with my husband's mother who graciously gave up her one bedroom and she slept in the lounge. My mother-in-law's residence was in an apartment block in an outer area of the capital and at the time had a library and one cafe I could visit if I managed to negotiate the unfamiliar slippery ice underneath the snow. The daylight was available for three hours and I knew one person, my husband. I would like to say I embraced my surroundings with an indomitable spirit. Unfortunately not, after a honeymoon period of about three weeks, reality set in and I began to wonder what the €#&# I was doing there. The pressure began to expose the cracks in my character and hidden fear and doubts began to surface. My wonderful pastors from New Zealand felt God was asking me two things,

"Who are you?"and "Do you love me?" These questions are pertinent. Did I know who I was in God and would I continue my love pursuit of him in spite of the pain and unknown. In the first months I needed antibiotics twice for infection, I felt nauseous often and my stomach wasn't well. I also started getting car sick which I had never had before. I had always hated it when something was wrong in my body and now, I was contending with this too on top of my emotional turmoil. I asked God,

"What do I have here?" I felt he replied,

"Love and opportunity" The one thing I was clinging to was my sense he was saying,

"I shouldn't land." I was to remain in the high place with him. The following summer after six months of staying with Mum we moved to the cottage in a bigger city. The change and the freedom of having my own space was comforting. I had discovered the causes of my physical issues and was doing much better and as I stood on the rock above our house overlooking the sea and to the city beyond, I felt hope stirring in my heart. I wrote this,

On the edge of the world
Flown on the wings of an eagle
Pink sky, white light
Warm wind blowing

Off the eagle's back
Where do I find myself
On a mountaintop
Surveying the land

Eyes scan the horizon
looking, watching, wondering
Courage in me questioning
Wisdom is beside me

I am not alone
Walking with me
We must sit and talk
So I wait
Still quiet on the mountain

In trust, in hope
Summer breeze blows
On the edge of the world

As we follow God, we enter the crucible of the fire.[127] We have touched on this already but God wanted me to burn hotter, the hotter the flame, the more impurities will come to the surface.

---

[127] See 1 Peter 1:3-7

Mine were coming up: fear, anxiety, self-doubt, insecurity. I thought we had already done a lot of character work in me, well it turns out, there is always more. As I was in a country where the first language is Finnish/Suomi; the isolation I experienced was heavy. Inner loneliness was a wound I already contended with and now I was in a situation that seemed to strike at it daily. I nor my husband had the energy to constantly keep up with translating everything for me and I retreated into a bitter shell and "sucked it up". It was though all my skills and who I was as a person were reduced to zero as I went back to school to learn Suomi. The walls come back, different walls but walls nonetheless. God encouraged me saying,

"I want to pour out all over you a never-ending river of divine presence; a constant in-filing.

Your life is about my goodness." I wasn't listening though, like Lot's wife[128] I kept looking back. I compared New Zealand with Finland, and I mourned. I didn't appreciate the good here. Yes, it was different but different is not bad. We have trouble with difference, our fear of difference is what fuels racism or sexism or any other group we could list. Holy Spirit said to me,

"Don't look back, shatter the self-reflecting mirror, Look to me!"

Every challenge or trial we go through is an opportunity to grow. God is not being mean. He is giving us our heart's desire for true rest and peace. It had been easier in New Zealand for my fears and insecurities to be masked, there I was in my comfort zone. One day as I was lying on my couch in the cottage I had an inner vision. I was in a heavenly place and there were people and angels standing in a circle giving attention to God on the throne. The perspective shifted, like a camera in a movie changing viewpoint. The scene was panned back, so instead of me looking at the scene through my first person perspective, the view became third person and I observed myself standing in the middle of the circle and God's throne was in the circle with the others.

---

[128] See Genesis 19:26

I gasped in horror, I wasn't supposed to be in the centre, Christ was! My selfishness and entitlement mentality were exposed. I often don't use this term due to its strength but this was and is satanic.

You said in your heart, "I will ascend to the heavens; I will raise my throne above the stars of God; I will sit enthroned on the mount of assembly, on the utmost heights of Mount Zaphon." Isaiah 14:13[129]

We are not the one on the throne. When life is all about me, I have placed myself in the centre. This is hard for some of us to face. Yes, I am valuable and important but I am not the most important. I belong to God, I belong to my community. I am one of many. We were created to receive attention and to be raised up. The only one who can and should do this is our great Father. In fact, he promises he will raise us up.

Humble yourselves before the Lord, and he will lift you up. James 4:10

My status as a foreign immigrant in Finland exposed many things in my heart. Father was kind to me, he did and has given me a group of amazing women from my husband's church who have become life-long friends and without them in the first years, I wouldn't have made it. They graciously took me in and loved this wild, New Zealand fireflower. However for me and this is not an accusation but my own subjective experience, the spiritual landscape was dry. Where was the prophetic? Where was the river of life flowing? Where could I find what I needed spiritually? It was at this point Holy Spirit said to me,

"Its not you, it's me. I flow through you. Will you pour yourself out even when you feel like nothing is coming in?" She led me back to these verses from scripture,

While the angel who was speaking to me was leaving, another angel came to meet him and said to him: "Run, tell that young man, 'Jerusalem will be a city without walls because of the great number of people and animals in it.

---

[129] As mentioned earlier some believe this a reference to Lucifer.

And I myself will be a wall of fire around it,' declares the LORD, 'and I will be its glory within.' Zechariah 2:3-5

God had already shown me the wall of fire around me and now he added to it, remember Jerusalem as well as being the actual city is also a metaphor for us. I was to be without walls with a great number of people and animals within me. In other words, I felt God telling me he was giving me the capacity to carry in my heart many people. Would I allow people to come and go? Would I serve people freely without walls or conditions? This would be a work of love and grace for it wasn't and isn't about me but him and his love flowing through me to people.

My verse for the coming Hebrew New Year exactly two years from when I was told a new season was beginning and I moved to Finland was,

Greater love has no one than this: to lay down one's life for one's friends. John 15:13

Would I enter into greater love? Would I call Finland my friend even though I felt isolated and second class? Would I give even as I felt nothing coming back in return? God kept reminding me of my freedom in him. I could bask in him on my mountain as much and as often as I wanted. There were no limitations for me in the spirit. My physical situation might be limited yet I was free and now there needed to an overflow from what I received from God to be given to others. I had the Source of all. I didn't need others to give me everything, I had everything in him. Father showed me what he was now going to do and it contained a promise. Only in hindsight do I more fully understand what was happening at this time,

"Therefore I am now going to allure her; I will lead her into the wilderness and speak tenderly to her. There I will give her back her vineyards, and will make the Valley of Achor[130] a door of hope. There she will respond[131] as in the days of her youth, as in the day she came up out of Egypt.

130 Achor means trouble
131 Or it could be translated sing

"In that day," declares the LORD, "you will call me 'my husband'; you will no longer call me 'my master. Hosea 2:14-15

God had called me into the wilderness to sit on the mountain in the spirit and be in the Valley of Achor (my place of trouble, see footnote below) in the natural. His promise was for it to become a door of hope, our relationship would change into one of greater intimacy. Simultaneously I heard the Spirit calling,

"The harvest is plentiful but the laborers are few."[132] Would I respond to his call and would I allow myself to face the greater depths in my soul of pain and fear?

[132] See Luke 10:2

CHAPTER 14

Facing the Fear

For those of us who have been raised in the Christian religion, there is a strong possibility we have been left with a deficit of love in our heart. This came as a revelation for me when I visited another country to attend a conference. During the worship I saw myself ascending a ladder, (I actually saw a picture my husband had drawn) the figure was weary. One of the visitors at the conference came to me and prayed for Jacob's ladder within me. I was to climb the stair. Through this picture I felt I received a download. In my teenage years I hadn't received the love of God into my heart, nor had I received the love of the world. I was loveless. We were created for love, for we were created by Love. This verse suddenly made sense to me,

I know your deeds, that you are neither cold nor hot. I wish you were either one or the other! So, because you are lukewarm—neither hot nor cold—I am about to spit you out of my mouth.

Revelation 3:15-16

God would rather we were cold towards him than lukewarm, my interpretation of this is if we are not getting the "heat" of God's presence, we need to get love from somewhere-the world. Being lukewarm even feels a bit gross thinking about it. Lukewarm baths means it's time to get out, lukewarm tea is kind of gross. And food when it is supposed to be served hot, isn't it a letdown when it comes out half cold compared to the pleasure of eating it piping hot? This shows too the measure of God's heart. He doesn't want a half-committed lover, could it be as distasteful to him as it is for us? When I think of myself, I need to know I'm the only one in my husband's life, I need him to be fixed on me, if he was to be lukewarm it would be devastating to my passionate heart. Some might say they don't need that kind of passion but if we were honest with ourselves, isn't it what we long for? Someone who adores us and is committed to us solely? And if we don't feel this way, is it possible we have walls protecting our hearts and hiding us from ourselves?

As I realised the deficit in me during the time of my teenage years, I felt God asking me to invite him into the loveless places. He wanted to fill that time of my life with his burning love and heal any rejection and isolation I had experienced due to religion where I didn't actually have the love of God and I didn't have the love of the world. God, the one who is outside of time can restore any moment in our lives and make it as though he was present there. Our memory of it stays but the stain and pain of the memory is washed new; to the memory of love eternal where we are filled to the measure of the fullness of God. As Paul writes,

I pray that out of his glorious riches he may strengthen you with power through his Spirit in your inner being, so that Christ may dwell in your hearts through faith. And I pray that you, being rooted and established in love, may have power, together with all the Lord's holy people, to grasp how wide and long and high and deep is the love of Christ, and to know this love that surpasses knowledge—that you may be filled to the measure of all the fullness of God. Ephesians 3:16-19

This loves stretches back through eternity to before time. Before you were conceived his love was there for you. As you were planted in your mother's womb through natural or scientific means, his love was there for you. As you were birthed into the world and took root in the soil of the earth growing from infancy to adolescence to adulthood, his love was there for you. He wants no part to be left without his love, there is no place where his love is not. As we are planted into the new soil, the new birth of life in Christ, this living love flows into every second of our lives. Receive this love now, he was with you, even when you were not with him for he steps in and has stepped in and did step in when we stepped into Christ. You are as a tree growing in the soil of love and his love came to this world, the moment Holy Spirit encountered the seed of Mary and fused together with humanity to be planted in the very same place we are all planted, earth.

My husband and I visited New Zealand. It had been three years since I had been home, the frailty of my humanity stared me in the face. I felt as though the ground beneath me was shaking and I had lost hold of my footing. Although seeing my family and friends was joyful I felt lost and confused. I didn't know where home was. In this shaking, I was taken back in time to the open heart surgery I had had at the age of seven. My parents had been told there were no guarantees my heart would start again after it had been stopped. I had a hole in my heart and it needed to be stitched up. The operation was originally intended to be done when I was a teenager but my health had deteriorated to the point where I was constantly ill and weak. Death hovered but in my picture, I saw a green (symbolising life) light — the Holy Spirit with me in the operating room, I heard her say,

"Your spirit never left the room for I was there." The cycle of life and death are constants here on earth. Right now as I type we are in the middle of the Covid-19 pandemic sweeping the world. Death knocks at our door, and no-one can escape, globally we are all in this boat together. Scripture says this,

Since the children have flesh and blood, he[133] too shared in their humanity so that by his death he might break the power of him who holds the power of death—that is, the devil—and free those who all their lives were held in slavery by their fear of death[134]. Hebrews 2:14-15

The fear of death is a root fear in all of us. One could say all fear stems from the fear of death. Take a moment, think of something you are afraid of. Why are you afraid? What happens if this occurs, what is the result? Jesus came to free us from being enslaved to the fear of death. We do die yet we rise again.

[133] He; meaning Christ
[134] Underlined for emphasis

Death is not a permanent state. When Christ rose from the grave he conquered death.

And when Jesus had cried out again in a loud voice, he gave up his spirit. At that moment the curtain of the temple was torn in two from top to bottom. The earth shook, the rocks split and the tombs broke open. The bodies of many holy people who had died were raised to life. They came out of the tombs after Jesus' resurrection and went into the holy city and appeared to many people. Mathew 27:50-53

We fear the unknown, death is unknown. As uncomfortable as it is, the ground beneath our feet is not solid. Earth does not provide us solidarity. It is hard to reconcile and I can understand the thinking that says, "When I die that's it, I return to the dust of the earth." There is a certain solidarity in this thought, a finality some find comfort in. I on the other hand am not comforted. I want to live, I want to exist and keep on existing, I want eternity. We have the promise of life,

On this mountain the LORD Almighty will prepare a feast of rich food for all peoples, a banquet of aged wine— the best of meats and the finest of wines. <u>On this mountain he will destroy the shroud that enfolds all peoples, the sheet that covers all nations; he will swallow up death forever.</u>[135] The Sovereign LORD will wipe away the tears from all faces; he will remove his people's disgrace from all the earth.

The LORD has spoken. Isaiah 25:6-8

On this mountain refers to those who have come into the kingdom, the mountain of Christ as referenced from Daniel. The shroud of death will be removed from us. It is a coming hope and it is a present reality as we step into the eternal realms of time.

For the perishable must clothe itself with the imperishable, and the mortal with immortality. When the perishable has been clothed with the imperishable, and the mortal with immortality, then the saying that is written will come true: "Death has been swallowed up in victory."

[135] Underlined for emphasis

"Where, O death, is your victory? Where, O death, is your sting?" The sting of death is sin, and the power of sin is the law. But thanks be to God! He gives us the victory through our Lord Jesus Christ. ! Corinthians 15:53-57

To allow death to lose its grip on me I needed to continue to confront my fears and admit to myself I was imprisoned. By nature, I am a sensitive person. Although I am joyful and outgoing in my relationships with people, I am a cautious person who does not "blindly run" into something. I will stop and think before I do something, especially something that may put me in physical danger. I dislike immensely contact sports. I like my body to be warm and safe. These are not bad characteristics and I have practiced pushing my boundaries, for example, going for a midnight swim in the ocean or deliberately putting myself in physically uncomfortable situations (Two weeks in the forest with no toilets or showers would count as such). We need cautious people in the world, we need all the personality types, however, my personality type is more easily prone to fear and fear seems to be a generational problem in my family line. We can grow up in a fear-filled atmosphere, for example with abusive or alcoholic parents, or having absent parents may cause fear due to a lack of feeling protected. There are many reasons why fear may dominate a household. These fears become a part of us and due to our own struggle with fear we "pass on" the atmosphere of fear to the next generation. We cannot give what we do not have, there is no condemnation in this. Father had been speaking to me for a long time about fear and ministering to me however now was the turning point. He had been teaching me to "feel the fear and do it anyway." I wanted more, I wanted to be free from the crippling and tormenting sensations of fear. I wanted to experience the peace of Christ promised to us. Not as a wishful thought but as an actual reality. I have learnt too it doesn't matter what our weaknesses, God will use these for good,

And we know that in all things God works for the good of those who love him, who have been called according to his purpose. Romans 8:28

In fact, our weaknesses become our strengths if we allow God to mould us. I now fiercely resist fear in all its forms being extremely sensitive to it, my fear has gradually turned into courage as I learn to overcome. My fears, wounds and sensitivity have been catalysts for me drawing near to God. I needed God to overcome, I needed him to lift me from my places of hopelessness. Psalm 40 was one of the first scriptures I held onto in the early years as I acknowledged God lifting me from destructive places.

I waited patiently for the LORD; he turned to me and heard my cry. He lifted me out of the slimy pit, out of the mud and mire; he set my feet on a rock and gave me a firm place to stand. He put a new song in my mouth, a hymn of praise to our God. Many will see and fear the LORD and put their trust in him. Blessed is the one who trusts in the LORD, who does not look to the proud, to those who turn aside to false gods. Many, LORD my God, are the wonders you have done, the things you planned for us. None can compare with you; were I to speak and tell of your deeds, they would be too many to declare. Sacrifice and offering you did not desire— but my ears you have opened— burnt offerings and sin offerings you did not require. Then I said, "Here I am, I have come— it is written about me in the scroll. I desire to do your will, my God; your law is within my heart." I proclaim your saving acts in the great assembly; I do not seal my lips, LORD, as you know. I do not hide your righteousness in my heart; I speak of your faithfulness and your saving help. I do not conceal your love and your faithfulness from the great assembly. Do not withhold your mercy from me, LORD; may your love and faithfulness always protect me. For troubles without number surround me; my sins have overtaken me, and I cannot see. They are more than the hairs of my head, and my heart fails within me. Be pleased to save me, LORD; come quickly, LORD, to help me. May all who want to take my life be put to shame and confusion; may all who desire my ruin be turned back in disgrace. May those who say to me,

"Aha! Aha!" be appalled at their own shame. But may all who seek you rejoice

and be glad in you; may those who long for your saving help always say, "The LORD is great!" But as for me, I am poor and needy; may the Lord think of me. You are my help and my deliverer; you are my God, do not delay. Psalm 40

This Psalm is prophetic for me and as I read it now it still speaks after 20 years of my life journey with God. What I want to highlight here though, is our need for deliverance. For those of you who feel weak, you are in the perfect place to receive from God. Your greatest weakness and fear is going to be turned into glory as you wait upon God to deliver you. We need only to have faith and endurance as we wait for the promise to be fulfilled.

Fear and anxiety plague many people in this age. In 2017, 284 million people worldwide were officially diagnosed with an anxiety disorder.[136] The World Health Organisation defines anxiety disorders in these terms,

"Anxiety disorders arise in a number of forms including phobic, social, obsessive compulsive (OCD), post-traumatic disorder (PTSD), or generalized anxiety disorders.

The symptoms and diagnostic criteria for each subset of anxiety disorders are unique. However, collectively the WHO's International Classification of Diseases (ICD-10) note frequent symptoms of:

"(a) apprehension (worries about future misfortunes, feeling "on edge", difficulty in concentrating, etc.);

(b) motor tension (restless fidgeting, tension headaches, trembling, inability to relax);

(c) autonomic overactivity (lightheadedness, sweating, tachycardia or tachypnoea, epigastric discomfort, dizziness, dry mouth, etc.)."[137]

Although I never had an official diagnosis regarding anxiety, I did I believe have mild episodes of panic attacks where I would experience some of the physical symptoms listed above.

---

[136] Hannah Ritchie and Max Roser (2020) - "Mental Health". Published online at OurWorldInData.org. Retrieved from: 'https://ourworldindata.org/mental-health' [Online Resource]
[137] Taken from the same source as above, footnote 133.

I also frequently worried about future misfortunes or had an illogical feeling of doom hanging over me like something bad was about to happen. A pastor once said fear could be defined as, "false evidence appearing real." This is an excellent acronym to describe fear. He went on to suggest that most of the time the fear does not materialise and the feeling of fear is often worse than the thing we fear actually happening.

As strange as this was, leaving New Zealand to go back to Finland was comforting. I had my little cottage on the edge of the world where I could hide away. Being in New Zealand was lovely but I felt overstimulated as I went through the deeper processes Holy Spirit had me in. Back on my cottage couch on a chilly March-day I tuned in online to a recorded church service. It wasn't a live stream. During the worship I saw a picture of a sphere of light around me. The main speaker took the microphone and the first words out of his mouth were,

"Did you know you have a sphere of light around you." If I hadn't have been sitting on my couch I would have fallen over, all my being was pulsating in anticipation for what the speaker would say next. He went on to explain that this is the light of Christ around us. It is also a protective atmosphere and I have authority over what comes into my space. He said whatever I focus my attention on is like a gateway and as I look at it, I invite whatever it is in.

We empower what we focus on. The words of Jesus about the eye being the lamp of the body make sense,

Your eye is the lamp of your body. When your eyes are healthy, your whole body also is full of light. But when they are unhealthy, your body also is full of darkness. Luke 11:34

Paul admonishes us to think about good things, what our gaze is fixed upon we think about and what we think about becomes a gateway for either light or dark to come in.

Finally, brothers and sisters, whatever is true, whatever is noble, whatever is

right, whatever is pure, whatever is lovely, whatever is admirable—if anything is excellent or praiseworthy—think about such things. Philippians 4:8

We have authority over ourselves, we have the mind of Christ. All the years I had spent training my mind (as much as I was able) to fix it on Christ, were training and preparation for my new freedom that was coming. I had spent years habitually dwelling on negative thoughts, partly due to the disposition of my character and partly due to the atmosphere of fear I had lived under without realising. The speaker went on to say the spirit of fear in itself was a small thing, the chain could easily be broken if we would remove our gaze from it and understand whose we are and who we are. This was the first step for me into freedom. Some days later I woke up with a strange image in my head. It has been normal for me over the years to wake up in the morning with a song in my head or a thought and I have learnt to pay attention to these as it is Holy Spirit speaking to me. He watches over us in the night watch and our spirit is in constant communion with him even if our consciousness is not.

For God does speak—now one way, now another— though no one perceives it. In a dream, in a vision of the night, when deep sleep falls on people as they slumber in their beds...Job 33:14-15

I woke to the image of the greek god Pan in my mind. I knew I had to do some research. Pan is half-man and half goat. In greek mythology Pan is known to go out into isolated places and harass the sheep and cause them to panic. The English word for panic has been taken from the greek god Pan. The definition of panic is this, *Sudden uncontrollable fear or anxiety, often causing wildly unthinking behaviour."*[138] The word's origin is, *"from French panique(15c.), from Greek panikon, literally "pertaining to Pan," the god of woods and fields, who was the source of mysterious sounds that caused contagious, groundless fear in herds and crowds, or in people in lonely spots."*[139]

[138] As defined by the dictionary.
[139] Taken from https://www.etymonline.com/search?q=panic.

As I pondered this information I heard Holy Spirit say to me,

"It is in isolated places where panic operates. Any isolated parts in your heart is where panic can reside. As you come out of isolation in your inner parts, panic will no longer have a place."

Now I understood why Father had been ministering to my heart and bringing memories and moments in time to the surface so his presence and love could fill those places. Remember our spirit is perfect in Christ as we stay joined to him, it is the soul; our heart, will and emotions which are in a process of transformation. Or as some would say, sanctification. Sanctify means, *to set apart to a sacred purpose or to religious use and to free from sin.*[140] Jesus prayed we would be sanctified,

For them I sanctify myself, that they too may be truly sanctified. John 17:19

Paul prays this also,

May God himself, the God of peace, sanctify you through and through. May your whole spirit, soul and body be kept blameless at the coming of our Lord Jesus Christ. 1 Thessalonians 5:23

Sanctification is not about becoming more pleasing to God, we already have his pleasure in Jesus. Rather it is about US being set free from bondage. My process was not making me holier, my process was setting me free from torment and lies. I now had the key to my panic, when I felt it coming I told my husband or I talked to Holy Spirit. I did not stay in my isolation and "suck it up because I should be strong and able to handle this." No, I admitted my weakness and allowed comfort to come to that place. Instead of fighting the fear, I acknowledged it was there and turned my face to love. I began a new way of dealing with it and as I did this, the stronghold of anxiety diminished. This did not happen all at once but over time as my brain created new neurological pathways. It is said it takes 21 times for a new habit to be established. As love comes it casts out fear, as fear leaves, the shadows of death leave with it.

[140] https://www.merriam-webster.com/dictionary/sanctifying

Life abundant promised to us is the life springing up from the inside of us to give us peace and joy.

As I sat in my car the other day waiting for my husband to come out of the grocery store, I felt so heavy due to the Covid-19 pandemic and the lockdown we were in. I opened my mouth to pray in tongues and I only got a few words out before a bubbling joy come up from within me and I started laughing. I literally felt the movement of Holy Spirit within me as her joy bubbled forth. Joy is listed as the second fruit of the Holy Spirit, followed by peace. It is not my job to manufacture fruit, they are the natural by-product of living in union with Holy Spirit as we dwell together. I can be stuck in my house for weeks and not have to succumb to the external fear, pressure and stress of the situation. As I continue to abide in Jesus I will experience a never-ending flow of love, joy, peace, patience, kindness, goodness, faithfulness, gentleness and self-control. No, I am not perfect in this, I experience the normal emotions of shock, worry and fear, but they do not rule me or take over as predominant emotions. As I am currently over 30-weeks pregnant it is essential I am in a peaceful state in spite of the pandemic. Holy Spirit knows this and comes as my helper. What a wonderful God we have who is able to do more than we can ask or imagine. I live a supernatural life! This is exactly the point, we live in eternal realms not confined to the realities of the material world. As we come out of fear into the arms of Love we find a freedom far greater than we have imagined. It is worth it to persevere. I encourage those of you who battle fear to not give up. Your victory is coming. I am in a different place than nine years ago and I can honestly say fear no longer has power over me, yes I feel fear but I am not imprisoned in my fear. Bye bye panic, greater glory has come.

And we all, who with unveiled faces contemplate the Lord's glory, are being transformed into his image with ever-increasing glory, which comes from the Lord, who is the Spirit. "Corinthians 3:18

CHAPTER 15

Divine Union

In these later years, quantum physics and more specifically quantum mechanics have spoken to me about the nature of God. God the greatest scientist reveals himself in these divine mysteries and theories. Take for instance the "double slit experiment"[141] where the photon acts like a wave and a particle. This led to the knowledge of electrons behaving in the same manner known as the wave- particle duality. In other words, the electron can materialise and dematerialise to be in two places at one time. Or quantum entanglement where two particles although in different locations are directly affected by the other. And where they communicate with one another at speeds greater than the speed of light. Even the infinity symbol, as featured on the cover, circles joined in unity ignites my mind to the expansiveness of who God really is. This does not intimidate me but excites me to learn more about this great God I am joined to. I am in quantum entanglement with God! For this last chapter, I felt God lead me to share three images of my relational change with God. It may not be this way for you but I do believe it highlights something in increasing intimacy and journeying with God as we accept his perpetual invitation to follow him. I want to start with Jacob who got his name changed to Israel,

So Jacob was left alone, and a man wrestled with him till daybreak. When the man saw that he could not overpower him, he touched the socket of Jacob's hip so that his hip was wrenched as he wrestled with the man. Then the man said, "Let me go, for it is daybreak." But Jacob replied, "I will not let you go unless you bless me."

141 Performed by Thomas Young in 1801

The man asked him, "What is your name?" "Jacob," he answered. Then the man said, "Your name will no longer be Jacob, but Israel, [142] *because you have struggled with God and with humans and have overcome." Jacob said, "Please tell me your name." But he replied, "Why do you ask my name?" Then he blessed him there. So Jacob called the place Peniel,* [143] *saying, "It is because I saw God face to face, and yet my life was spared." The sun rose above him as he passed Peniel, and he was limping because of his hip.*

Genesis 32:24-31

Notice the first words, **So Jacob was left alone.** We alone walk with God. No person is there to hold our hand. This is likely the first and greatest barrier for some. It takes courage to leave the crowd and be left alone to contend with God. God came to Jacob as a man, just as Christ came as a man.

God comes to us in a way we can understand, he limits himself as we begin to take hold of him. In the early days of my relationship with God, I wrestled. This is a necessary and blessed place. I would dare say this, God WANTS us to wrestle with him. It is a way of knowing him and as I have shared it removes questions and barriers as we push against God seeking to trust how good he really is. Ask for God's blessing in your life, do not settle for less, step into the arena and wrestle with him even as Jacob did. Jacob did not even know his name. This is true for us as well. Knowing someone's name especially in ancient cultures revealed something about the person's character. This is seen throughout scripture, what we name we give importance to and define who or what they are. If you don't know God's name you are in good company with Jacob. God is looking at our motives just as he asked Jacob, **"Why do you ask my name?"** Yet God honoured Jacob's desire and blessed him although this was not without consequences. He touched Jacob in such a way that Jacob was left with a limp. We are not the same after we wrestle with God.

---

[142] Israel means he struggles with God
[143] Peniel means face of God

We lose our full strength and capacity. There is greater purpose in losing our own strength. Not only do we lose our capacity, we change. Jacob got a name change, his identity was shifting. As we wrestle with God our identity changes. The last line of the above scriptures sums up Jacob's experience beautifully and gives a hint of what is coming in his future. ***The sun rose above him as he passed Peniel, and he was limping because of his hip.*** As I read this sentence, I felt Holy Spirit read it to me this way,

"The Son (Christ) rose above him as he passed the face of God and he was limping."

What happens when we limp? We need something or someone to lean upon and this transition leads us to the next phase in our God relationship.

Friends: Who is this coming up from the wilderness leaning on her beloved? Song of Solomon 8:5

As I was led into the wilderness, I limped, I had been wrestling with God. I limped due to religious burnout, I limped in my weaknesses as I acknowledged my powerlessness. In my limping I needed to lean, I began to lean into Christ. Only he could sustain me. It is here I learnt like the Apostle John to recline on the one I loved. In this place, the heartbeat of God came into focus. If you are limping embrace it, it is your doorway into the greatest intimacy you have yet known. Make friends with your limp, rejoice in it as Paul rejoiced in his weaknesses.

The song of songs is a love story and it shows a progression of love maturing. Real love goes through several stages. Real love is tested. Real love gives the other free will to depart until consummation is complete and Jesus the bridegroom says to us,

Fasten me upon your heart as a seal of fire forevermore. This living consuming flame will seal you as my prisoner of love. My passion is stronger than the chains of death and the grave, all- consuming as the very flashes of fire from the burning heart of God. Place this fierce, unrelenting fire over your entire being. Rivers of pain and persecution with never extinguish this flame. Endless floods will be unable to quench this raging fire that burns within you. Everything will be consumed. It will stop at nothing as you yield everything to this furious fire until it won't seem to you like a sacrifice anymore. Song of Songs 8:6-7 TPT[144]

It is at this point that no matter what happens in my life whether good or bad, I will not depart from my Jesus. I may not understand but my heart is set, I may be like a fire where the flames diminish and it smoulders. Onlookers might think the flame has died but no, if one were to stoke the flame it would come alive. If one were to pour cold water on it, it would supernaturally remain smouldering. And the fury of love would rise again from the ashes like the phoenix bird, resurrected for another thousand years. I have taken root and this love cannot die, this body will die and Love will resurrect it. You see it is Love in the end which resurrects us and it is wholly our choice if we reciprocate this love.

We are not finished yet. It is not enough to be leaning on the beloved, I want full union. I hunger to be one with God. God is one,

Hear, O Israel: The Lord our God, the Lord is one. Deuteronomy 6:4

Union with himself is the divine mystery; Father, Son and Holy Spirit. It doesn't stop there, we are invited into this oneness as Jesus prayed,

I pray also for those who will believe in me through their message, that all of them may be one, Father, just as you are in me and I am in you. May they also be in us so that the world may believe that you have sent me. I have given them the glory that you gave me, that they may be one as we are one—I in them and you in me—so that they may be brought to complete unity. Then the world will know that you sent me and have loved them even as you have loved me. John 17:20.23

---

[144] Scripture quotations marked TPT are from The Passion Translation®. Copyright © 2017, 2018 by Passion & Fire Ministries, Inc. Used by permission. All rights reserved. ThePassionTranslation.com.

The divine mystery continues in us as we enter God and become his substance. It is not only a partnership, it is quite literally union. This is not a picture or metaphor, this is a real place IN Christ. We eat his flesh and drink his blood. His substance becomes our substance. Our time dimension blurs our understanding, yes I am already in Christ and I am becoming one with Christ. I am already married to Christ yet I am still waiting for the marriage celebration.[145]

The greatest union awaits us all, as WE, beloveds of Jesus are bought to complete unity. As this happens the world will know the Father sent Jesus and loves us. We are not alone inside the union, we are accompanied by others! Does this not trigger echoes of one of God's initial declarations, *"It is not good for man to be alone."*[146] We can see how desperate people are not to be lonely, think about the upsurge of polyamorous relationships, or open relationships. Are these shadows of what the heart is really longing for? Could it be we are looking for this grand union? It is not my intention here to delve into cultural trends but I want to speak to the wise and discerning; what is the reason behind gender confusion, why are we searching for more beyond the traditional one man and one woman relationships? Why are we "breaking the rules?" Are we straining to reach beyond the shadows of this world before its appointed time into the eternal realm?[147] Where there is no gender, no separation from another, no hatred, no loneliness. In the eternal realm there is Love in perfect unity. Unity is not conformity, Love is diverse, Love does not have hierarchy[148]. WOW. Isn't this what we are really longing for? With all my heart I believe the next move of God is to manifest this union in us. It will no longer be the one great leader or a few leaders the church recognises Christ the shepherd in and follows.

[145] See Revelation 19:7
[146] See Genesis 2:18
[147] Author disclaimer; I am not advocating "breaking the rules" as established by Father in this earth/time dimension. But I am suggesting a reason for what we see in society. In the hearts of all humanity are whispers of the truth of the eternal realm, without the light and truth of Christ it would be easy for these whispers to be distorted. And yes Father has set the lonely in families in the boundaries established by him.
[148] See Luke 22:24-26

It will be a company of people, the corporate bride rising up as one, each marked with their own identity in Christ yet each in harmony with the other. We see this prophetically foretold,[149]

Moses then took the blood, sprinkled it on the people and said, "This is the blood of the covenant that the LORD has made with you in accordance with all these words." Moses and Aaron, Nadab and Abihu, and the seventy elders of Israel went up and saw the God of Israel. Under his feet was something like a pavement made of lapis lazuli, as bright blue as the sky. But God did not raise his hand against these leaders of the Israelites; they saw God, and they ate and drank.

Exodus 24:8-11

After blood had been shed, not just Moses but a whole company of leaders saw God. They ate and drank, this symbolises fellowship. This is a clear foretelling of the shed blood of Christ, the only way by which we can see God. Jesus too said we must eat and drink of him. It doesn't specify exactly what they ate. It may well have been actual food but does it not hint at "eating and drinking God"? Originally God wanted all of Israel to have access to him, he had called them all to the mountainside to hear his voice when Moses went to receive the ten commandments yet they rejected God in this moment. Moses recounted the incident back to the people,

When you heard the voice out of the darkness, while the mountain was ablaze with fire, all the leaders of your tribes and your elders came to me. And you said, "The LORD our God has shown us his glory and his majesty, and we have heard his voice from the fire. Today we have seen that a person can live even if God speaks with them. But now, why should we die? This great fire will consume us, and we will die if we hear the voice of the LORD our God any longer. For what mortal has ever heard the voice of the living God speaking out of fire, as we have, and survived? Go near and listen to all that the LORD our God says. Then tell us whatever the LORD our God tells you. We will listen and obey." Deuteronomy 5:23-27

---

[149] I need to again credit Michael Fickess for teaching this.

This text hidden in scripture reveals a profound truth. God did not want Moses to be the go-between person between himself and the community. He wanted all the people to hear him for themselves. It was the Israelite community that pushed God away and asked for Moses to speak to God for them. We can see God's heart saddened by this throughout the story of the wandering Israelites. God felt their rejection, there were times when he said things like,

Then the LORD said to Moses, "Go down, because your[150] people, whom you brought up out of Egypt, have become corrupt. Exodus 32:7

God called the people, "Moses's people", not his own. Of course in this context, they had been found worshipping the golden calf, something that had been expressively forbidden. God was angry however the people had already distanced themselves from God in their fear as we read above. This wrong kind of fear will always drives us away from God. We can't love someone we are afraid of.

The greater point I want to make is, it was always God's heart to take the whole community to himself. Now is the time when God's heart's desires are coming true as each of us can hear God for ourselves without having an intermediary and we are gathered together as a whole, not solely as individuals. In this hour Holy Spirit is restoring community, we cannot have true union with God without being in union with one another. This will be a main focus in the coming generations. God does want a one world order, an order where he reigns as King! There is only one kingdom which will ultimately stand in the end, the kingdom of Christ. Until then as Jesus said, the wheat will grow alongside the weeds, meaning the true lovers of Jesus will grow together with those who are not and all the counterfeit plans with it .[151] Unity is in God's heart for the days ahead and those of us who come to the place where we are done with wrestling with him and have become still so as to lean into him and hear his heart will hear the call,

[150] Underlined for emphasis
[151] See Mathew 13:30

"Come into me and bring the others with you."

For us to experience true union with God we will be in unity with others. I had been asking God the question, "How do I eat your body Jesus, how do I drink your blood?" What I was looking for was the practical application. This question was in response to these scriptures,

Jesus said to them, "Very truly I tell you, unless you eat the flesh of the Son of Man and drink his blood, you have no life in you. Whoever eats my flesh and drinks my blood has eternal life, and I will raise them up at the last day. For my flesh is real food and my blood is real drink.

Whoever eats my flesh and drinks my blood remains in me, and I in them. John 6:53-56

I know we take communion in our services, but there was something more to this. Recently during worship in a leaders's conference, I had a mental image where I saw myself lying flat on bare soil. As I lay on the ground I began to eat the earth. I pondered what it meant as the worship continued.

Adam the first human was created from the dust/dry soil. Earth represents humanity. The name Adam in Hebrew means: dust, clay, earth, mud. Jesus became human[152], he became earth. Those who receive Christ become his body. We as Jesus's followers are his body. To eat something means to assimilate it, what we eat becomes one with us. That substance becomes part of our physical body. From this action of eating earth, I understood to eat Jesus's body means I must assimilate earth; humanity. I must take humanity into myself, go lower, serve and become one with others, especially the church Christ's body. Earth might not taste pleasant. This is the point, for us to be fully united with Christ, we must also be united with our own humanity and with others. It doesn't always feel pleasant, or look pretty. It is dirty and raw and sometimes foul or smelly. This is our invitation, eternal life will flow in me as I embrace the fullness of what it means to be created from earth.

[152] See John 1:14

I do not escape this world I embrace it. I do not escape the "dirt" of being in union with others, instead I take that dirt into myself and I drink the blood of Jesus his life, his grace. Although I eat that which might not be nice, I also get to drink that which has the full power of life and glory in it, the blood of Christ. The blood poured into the earth at the foot of the cross from which hangs divine love. It is at this place where I lay. Let us lay on this piece of earth and feel the divine love pouring over us as we allow ourselves to be human, as we give of ourselves to others, as we allow our own flesh to be torn and given away that others may receive life. We come into Christ by serving others and allowing ourselves to be like Christ, love poured out.

We are sacred ground, for those of us who come into Christ become as he is. We are holy temples rising upwards into eternity made for the praise of his glory. Every piece of us illuminates his goodness. Every drop of blood in us sings of his reality. Every breath in, we breathe him in, every breath out we declare victory. In us, earth and heaven are united as we walk with Jesus. Love this earth beloveds, love it into wholeness in all its dirt and injustice. Humanity is holy. Join in the groan of all creation and become the caretaker of redemption. We climb the stair (Christ), ascending and descending from earth to heaven and back again. The stairway Jacob saw would have looked like a stairway from an ancient ziggurat.

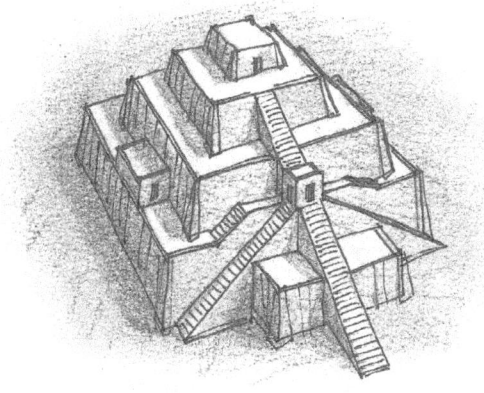

He had a dream in which he saw a stairway resting on the earth, with its top reaching to heaven, and the angels of God were ascending and descending on it. Genesis 28:12

The ancients in Mesopotamia believed the higher up you could get, the better the gods would be able to hear you. Each city would have a temple ziggurat. It would be the highest building in the town. Ziggurats did not have internal chambers but stairs reaching to the shrine at the top. Jacob called the stairway he saw the house of God and the gate of heaven,

He was afraid and said, "How awesome is this place! This is none other than the house of God; this is the gate of heaven." Genesis 28:17

With Jesus we have become the house of God and the gate of heaven. We are the gate love flows through as we learn to love God, love ourselves and love others. The whole of the cosmos is waiting for us to become one with Love Divine: Father, Son and Holy Spirit. Oh God make me one with you.

Ziggurat
In the bowels of the deep
In the dark
There begins a stair
It rises up
Curving around
From the depths
It climbs
ascending into the light
rising higher and higher
Shadows fade away
To the top I have not yet climbed
I am steadily moving forward
One step at a time

The stair is in me

A ziggurat of glory

The joy of the Father

A ladder of victory

Angels will traverse the stair

Jesus the first stairway journeys with me

His delight upon me

His radiance my peace

This ziggurat will worship

Intense burning

Holy desire

Only the true dares to come

Courage to be the ziggurat for my God

Come and dwell on me, in me.

Make your home in this temple dedicated to you alone

My King, my heart, my fire

Help me reach higher levels

realms of glory where your throne abides

In the highest place with priestly access I come

To see your face

Hear your voice

Know your ways

Reflect your will-realignment

Transfer your power

Give gifts to the poor

Shine your light

In the dark

Back at the bottom of the stair

In the bowels of the deep

This ziggurat.

About the Author

At the age of seventeen Jenna gave herself to God; willing to die as a foreign missionary if necessary. What transpired however has been a life of adventure as Holy Spirit beckoned her to follow the way of love, beginning in her home country of New Zealand. From bible college to journalism school to leadership training through to teaching English as a Foreign language she now resides in Finland with her Finnish husband and daughter. The adventure continues as she writes, teaches and preaches what she hears and sees coming from the Father's heart. Jenna found Christ to be wilder and greater than she could possibly ever have imagined. Her heart is to tell the final fairytale where we do live happily ever after.

Social Media: https://youtube.com/@descendlow?si=gYfCQLg9hFhX_xkI

Email: jenna.hastelow@gmail.com

SeraphCreative

Heaven's Heart for Earth

Seraph Creative is a collective of artists, writers, theologians & illustrators who desire to see the body of Christ grow into full maturity, walking in their inheritance as Sons Of God on the Earth.

Sign up to our newsletter to know about the release of new books by Ron Jones as well as other exciting releases.

Visit our website :

www.seraphcreative.org

www.ingramcontent.com/pod-product-compliance
Lightning Source LLC
Chambersburg PA
CBHW051518120626
46551CB00012B/983